I0013999

Social Media Roadmap: Navigating New Strategies for Small Businesses
Beth Schillaci

VillageWorks Communications, Inc.
PO Box 555
Frederick, MD 21705

copyright © 2010 Beth Schillaci

Book Design: Three Old Souls

Book Website: www.yoursocialmediaroadmap.com

Notice of Rights
All rights reserved. No part of this book may be reproduced or transmitted in any form by any means, electronic, mechanical, photocopying, recording, or otherwise, without prior written permission.

Notice of Liability
The information in this book is distributed on an "As Is" basis without warranty. While every precaution has been taken in the preparation of this book, the author shall not have any liability to any person or entity with respect to any loss or damage caused or alleged to be caused directly or indirectly by the instructions contained in this book or by the computer software and websites described in it.

Trademarks
Many of the designations used by companies to distinguish their products or services are claimed as trademarks. Where those designations appear in the book, the author was aware of a trademark claim, the designations appear as as requested by the owner of the trademark. All other product names and services identified throughout this book are used in editorial fashion only and for the benefit of such companies with no intention of infringement of the trademark. No such use, or the use of any trade name, is intended to convey endorsement or other affiliation with this book.

First Printing: 2010

ISBN: 1453821945
Library of Congress Control Number: 2010913797

Printed in the United States of America

Your
Social Media
Roadmap

Navigating New Strategies for Small Businesses

....

Beth Schillaci

TABLE OF CONTENTS

FOREWORD

Small Business Success Index™ (SBSI), sponsored by Network Solutions® and the University of Maryland's Smith School of Business, reports social media adoption by small businesses has doubled from 12 to 24 percent in the last year. The SBSI found that nearly one out of five small business owners are actively using social media. Small businesses are increasingly investing in social media applications including blogs, Facebook, and LinkedIn profiles—an indication of the landscape of small business marketing today. With social networks like Facebook reporting an audience of more than 500 million, you have to start the process of adding these tools into your marketing strategy—whether you are selling gifts, food, or services.

This book shows you how.

I met Beth Schillaci IRL (In Real Life) when I was a keynote speaker at the New Media & Technology Conference organized by the Frederick Chamber of Commerce in February 2010. Before this meeting I had known Beth virtually on Twitter and through her blog http://marketingroadhouse.com/. We share similar interests in educating small business owners about how to add social media tools and create a new Internet marketing strategy.

Being a small business owner herself, and having several years of experience in marketing, Beth understands the puzzlement of small businesses struggling to find meaning in the new Internet marketing maze. She has presented to several audiences on how to get started with social media, and she recently hosted a Network Solutions' Small Business tweetchat on "Blogging Effectively to Market Your Business."

Beth has written this book as a step-by-step process for owners of new and established small businesses to implement and execute a strategy for their business. She benchmarks her success when her clients, with a little training and direction, feel truly empowered to interact with their audience in an effective manner.

Beth not only advises businesses on the use of social media, but she also uses it herself to grow her business. Beth is proud of the connections she has made through the use of social media and has met business partners, clients, and many smart people who have enriched her personal and business life. This book reflects those networking successes as well.

Shashi Bellamkonda
"Social Media Swami"
Network Solutions

WHAT TO EXPECT

This book came into existence because I decided to write down the start-to-finish process I use to help my clients integrate social media into their marketing plans. I never imagined it would result in enough information to fill a book, but here you are reading it.

What I have created is a roadmap to guide you through creating and implementing your social media marketing strategy. It is not a "How to Use Facebook and Twitter" book but rather a way for you to understand and create your own strategy for using these tools. Only you truly know what is best for your company. It is my goal to guide you through the decision-making process so that you can create the plan that's right for you.

This book is not only for those who are new to using social media for business marketing. It's also for those who have been using pieces of social media but now want to create an overall strategy to put all of the pieces together. Using the pieces may be working well for you, but putting them into an overall strategy with the rest of your marketing can make you more effective.

While the book does follow a step-by-step process, each chapter can be read separately. I anticipate that each reader will use this book differently. Some of you will read it from front to back, while others will jump around to get the specific information you need. As you go, you'll be writing notes for your strategy, so you'll want to keep this book handy as a reference in the future.

If you are involved in a non-profit organization, this book has value for you as well. Just swap the terms customers with donors or volunteers and sales with donations to make the information apply to your social media marketing needs.

Who I am

I am a small business owner just like you. After working for many software start-ups, I decided to start my own business in 1999. For the past 11-plus years I have been working with other small businesses to help them utilize the Internet for marketing. My focus started with websites of all shapes and sizes and has evolved to now include social media and other digital strategies.

I understand where you are coming from because I'm there with you. As a small business owner, you wear many hats and never have enough resources to complete everything you want to get done. I wrote this book from one small business owner to another. I tried to keep things short and sweet because I know you don't have a lot of time to read. I also tried to give you enough actionable information so you can hit the ground running with a complete strategy when you finish reading the last page.

What you will find

➤ Getting Back to (Marketing) Basics

This overview of marketing concepts serves as your refresher course, as well as a comparison of marketing before and after social media. This chapter gets you back to thinking about marketing basics.

➤ Evaluating Where You Are Now

This chapter walks you through evaluating your current marketing strategy, your Unique Selling Proposition, and your competition. By looking at all 4 P's of marketing, you can see what you are currently doing so that you can make informed decisions about your social media strategy.

➤ Taking Inventory of Your Current Tools

Social media does not stand alone from your other marketing tools, so this chapter helps you evaluate your current marketing tools. By looking at what works and what doesn't, you can make decisions on how to make time for adding social media to your mix.

➤ Planning Where You Want to Go

Without knowing your target market and the message you want to deliver to that audience, you have no idea whether or not you achieve your goals. This chapter prepares you to move forward with your social media strategy.

➤ Setting Up Your Listening Post

The first step of any effective social media strategy is listening. This chapter gives you an understanding of why listening is so important and then provides information on how to establish your listening post.

➤ You're Listening. Now What?

Once your listening post is up and running, you will collect a lot of data. This chapter shows you how to pull important information from that data.

➤ Preparing for Worst-Case Scenario

When involved in social media, you open yourself up to certain risks. The best thing you can do is prepare for these situations before engaging. If a situation occurs, you won't be caught by surprise and you'll know exactly what to do.

➤ Choosing the Right Tools for the Job

To execute your social media strategy, you need to use the best tools for the job. This chapter's overview of available tools helps you decide what to put in your social media toolbox.

➤ Putting It All Together

After selecting the tools, it is time to put them together into a cohesive strategy and plan. In this chapter, you make the final selection of your tools and define your audience, message, and goals for each tool.

➤ Implementing the Tools

This chapter helps you get your tools set up and working. Checklists and tools that can help you manage your accounts are also discussed.

➤ Putting the Plan into Action

In this chapter, you learn some ways to get organized and stay on track when creating content and managing your accounts.

➤ Promoting Your Social Media Efforts

What is the purpose of all your social media work if no one knows about it? This chapter covers how to let people know about your efforts both online and off.

➤ Measuring Results

Find out how to measure your social media efforts in order to make decisions about moving forward or changing direction.

➤ Call-outs

Throughout the book, you will find call-outs to provide more information beyond creating your plan, including:

Potholes – These help you to avoid some of the most common mistakes that people engaging in social media often make. While they are also referenced within the text of the book, I think it is important to call them out as well. I want you to have a smooth ride.

Tales from the Road – I surveyed small business owners just like you. They have tackled social media on their own and are willing to share their stories with you. Remember, you are not alone.

Map Legend – When I use a word or concept that may be new to you, I call out the definition right on the page so there is no flipping to a glossary in the back.

....

It's time to fasten your seatbelt, and let's hit the road.

Be sure to check out the book's website at www.yoursocialmediaroadmap.com for updates.

....

TALES FROM THE ROAD

Innovative Career Consulting, Inc.
www.innovativecareerconsulting.com

WHAT HAS BEEN YOUR BIGGEST SUCCESS?

As a new business, our biggest success has been the rate at which we were able to create and build our brand in the Denver market using social media. I am still amazed at the access we have to our clients, potential clients, influencers, industry experts, the media covering our industry, and our competitors. Clearly, social media has played a vital role in allowing us to gather information in days that would normally take months and months.

Our company is now on people's radar screens after seven months in business. This is not something that could have happened five years ago.

ANY ADVICE FOR BUSINESSES JUST GETTING STARTED WITH SOCIAL MEDIA?

Don't try and learn everything overnight. Take baby steps. Make sure you have a solid foundation for your social media plans; otherwise, you are putting a good plan on top of a bad one. Lastly, do your homework. Find out from other like-minded people what works, what doesn't work, and what you need to incorporate into your social media plan. Most people are happy to help. All you need to do is ask.

WHAT WAS YOUR BIGGEST FEAR BEFORE STARTING WITH SOCIAL MEDIA – AND WAS THE FEAR WARRANTED?

My biggest fear was that social media was going to be one big waste of my time—time that I didn't have to waste. It was completely unwarranted. Social media is all about the changing way that people are communicating with each other. If we're not part of the conversation now, we will miss out on some great opportunities.

GETTING BACK TO (MARKETING) BASICS

Because your social media strategy should not stand on its own, you need a clear understanding of marketing. Marketing is the activity, set of institutions, and processes for creating, communicating, delivering, and exchanging offerings that have value for customers, clients, partners, and society at large. [1]

That's a lot of words and, even with a marketing degree, I have some trouble digesting that explanation. Plainly said, when you "market something" you provide products or services to the audience who wants and/or needs them. People often think that marketing is pushing a product or service so that someone buys it—but, at its core, marketing is truly about developing a product or service the audience wants. If the audience doesn't want or need your product or service, they won't buy it.

Let's clear up a common misconception. Advertising is not marketing; however, advertising is one small aspect of marketing. Marketing consists of the Four P's: Product, Price, Place, and Promotion. Advertising falls under Promotion, the aspect of marketing with which most people are familiar.

Let's look at each of these Ps in more detail and see how social media can affect each one.

[1] American Marketing Associations Board of Directors (Approved October 2007)
http://www.marketingpower.com/aboutama/pages/definitionofmarketing.aspx

Product

Product is the actual product and/or service that you sell. It includes all the features, functions, and benefits derived from using it. Beyond that, your product includes the packaging you use and any warranties and service you provide after the sale.

Customer research can help you better understand what your customer wants most. This research can be formal and often costly—with market research and focus groups—or more casual with simple surveys of people you know in your target market or current customers.

With social media, you have the ability to gain opinion and market research for almost free, compared to traditional market research. Online suggestion boxes enable your customers to ask questions and provide feedback on improvements or new features. You can also ask directly for feedback on social networks. I know this great local toy store that uses <u>Twitter</u> and <u>Facebook</u> to post pictures of products they are thinking of carrying to gauge interest.

Incredible Technologies, creator of the Golden Tee golf video game, has even gone as far as adding social media directly into its product. If you make a virtual hole-in-one on Golden Tee, you can share the video of the

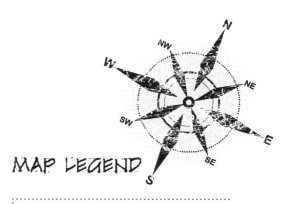

MAP LEGEND

TWITTER is a micro-blogging tool because it limits posts to 140 characters. It allows you to connect with people and companies in real-time conversations. **www.twitter.com**

FACEBOOK is a social network used by more than 500 million people worldwide. Facebook gives you many options to connect with its users, including pages, applications, and advertising. **www.facebook.com**

"Great Shot" with your friends by loading it directly to YouTube from the game. In just one year, more than 70,000 Great Shots have been uploaded.

Price

Price is what you charge for your product and/or service, as well as any discounts you offer or special pricing for bundling products and services.

Other factors figure into pricing. How much does it cost to buy or manufacture the product? What is the competition charging? What will the market bear? What will the margins be?

Social media gives you some great opportunities for trying different pricing and discounts. You can provide your most loyal customers who engage in social media with a special price or coupon. Perhaps you could offer an early-bird special or a discount to move extra inventory exclusively to your loyal community.

Starbucks is one of many companies that use Foursquare to reward its loyal customers by giving the Mayor a one-dollar discount on a drink. These Mayors are the people who visit most often and are truly engaged with the brand.

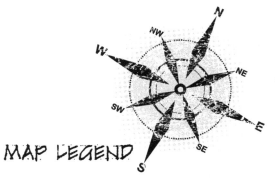

MAP LEGEND

YOUTUBE is an online video community owned by Google, with approximately 2 billion videos viewed per day. Videos hosted on YouTube can be shared on other social sites or embedded on your blog.
www.youtube.com

FOURSQUARE is a location-based social network that allows users to check in at locations they visit. The more you visit, the more likely you are to become Mayor. People can participate with no involvement from the business.
www.foursquare.com

Place

Place refers to the channel you use to deliver your product or service to customers. Your distribution channel is how you put your product into your customers' hands.

Traditional methods of distribution are direct and indirect sales—direct meaning that you sell directly to the customer through your own sales force, a store, or even online, and indirect meaning that you use an intermediary (such as a wholesaler or reseller) to resell your product or service. Some businesses use a combination of direct and indirect sales.

Social media can provide a new "place" to sell and even deliver your product or service to your customer. Consider these two examples:

- Dell Computers offers outlet pricing through its Twitter feed and has sold more than $6 million in computer products via Twitter in the last few years.

- Although Pizza Hut already had online ordering through its website, the company created a Facebook application for ordering pizza. Pizza Hut created this application because it learned that its target audience (college students) does not like to leave their Facebook accounts to order pizza, so they brought the ordering to the audience.

Businesses in all shapes and sizes can find opportunities to more effectively reach prospective and current customers in the places where they already spend their time.

Promotion

Promotion is how you tell people about your product or service so they know what it is (product), how much it costs (price), and where to buy it (place).

Promotion has traditionally included advertising and public relations. Advertising is typically done through some kind of media, namely newspapers, magazines, radio, television, online, and direct mail. Public relations refers to your relationship with the press and how you distribute news about your product and company to them.

Social media has increased the ability to promote your company, product, or service very effectively and efficiently. You can take your message directly to your target market and get a fairly immediate response. The feedback you receive can be critical to making smart, informed business decisions.

Ford Motor Cars is a very social media savvy company and decided to unveil the newly redesigned 2011 Ford Explorer on its own Facebook page. Ford posted videos leading up to the event to build upon the excitement. Though the launch is finished, people are still sharing their thoughts and opinions with the company on the page.

As you can see, social media has impacted how companies approach the 4 Ps. Now let's take a look at some other ways marketing has changed due to social media.

Marketing then

Many businesses still use the traditional tried-and-true methods of marketing that worked in the past—even though their audiences have moved on in terms of how they interact with brands.

➤ One-way, controlled communications

Marketing was considered a one-way communications tool. Companies pushed their message out to the public and assumed that message was what the public would believe.

Because companies pushed out this one-way communication, they felt they had control over their messages. They sent press releases that showed up as stories in magazines and newspapers. There was no way for people to comment on or question these stories, other than in casual conversation or with small groups.

➤ Message for the masses

In the past, a company's message was delivered to everyone and not targeted at smaller niche markets—mostly because of price. It was cost prohibitive to customize messages to each target market. Because of the high cost of advertising nationally, most marketing was limited to local or regional media choices.

➤ Campaign-based marketing

Most marketing and advertising was based on a campaign. Remember the Nike Air Jordan commercials with Michael Jordon and Spike Lee or the Federal Express ads with the fast talker? Some campaigns were seasonal due to the product, such as the Hess Truck ads every Christmas, and others delivered a certain story to the audience. It was very difficult for businesses to maintain an ongoing marketing message for an extended amount of time.

➤ Limited word of mouth

Word-of-mouth marketing was limited to small groups at the office, bus stop, or book club. In the past, if someone had a positive experience, they would tell five people, while if they had a negative experience they would tell twice as many—or more. The good news was that bad experiences would reach that group of people and then blow over. The bad news was that the same thing would happen with good experiences, but the number of people in the discussion was often fewer. Companies had no way of knowing about these conversations—and had no ability to respond or share information.

Marketing now

➤ Two-way conversations

Social media has created a two-way conversation between companies and their audience. The many tools that facilitate the conversation will change and evolve over time, but the conversation remains the same. With social media in your marketing mix, you can learn from your audience and respond to any issues, complaints, and compliments.

Dell Computers has a site called IdeaStorm (http://www.ideastorm.com) that allows the public to make suggestions on how to improve Dell's products and customer service. The best part is that Dell listens and incorporates many of the requested changes.

➤ Able to target audience—and message

Through monitoring and research, you can identify where your target market "hangs out" online, which enables you to set up accounts in the appropriate places and engage with your prospective and current customers. Once you locate your audience, you can effectively deliver a very specific message. Different audiences will require different messages, which are now easier and more affordable to deliver with all the available tools at your disposal.

Ford, as another example, manages several pages on Facebook. Each page is for a different model and in addition to the main corporate page. The company understands that its audience may only be interested in one model, so Ford accommodates that with a different and specific message to each audience.

➤ Strategy- and campaign-based marketing

You can use social media to promote a campaign, but it is equally effective as an ongoing communication and marketing tool. By managing an ongoing communication strategy, you are better able to stay "top of mind" with your audience. People will think of your company first when they need your product or service.

Pennfield Equine, manufacturer of horse feed, has a Facebook page for ongoing communications with its audience. To augment the ongoing strategy, the company ran a six-week trivia contest on its website that was promoted via Facebook and Twitter.

➤ Less control, more opportunity

With social media, your message can take on a life of its own very quickly, which is not always a bad thing. Your audience can evangelize and promote for you as well. If a customer has an issue, you can respond and turn that person into a satisfied champion of your company. There are several successful Facebook pages created by people who love a specific product or company. Use your raving fans to your advantage.

Coca-Cola's Facebook page was created by two people who love the products and not by the company. Coke was smart not to try and have the page shut down, but leaving it under the ownership of the creators and then partnering with the creators to be contributors to the page.

➤ Unlimited word of mouth

With social media, your company's "reach" is much larger. Word-of-mouth marketing has more of a ripple effect than ever before; not only is information easily shared with your own network, but individual members of your network can also share information with their networks. People connect with others who are like-minded on social networks, so what may be of interest to one is probably going to interest many within that network.

➤ Full transparency

Gone are the days when companies could send out a message they couldn't really stand behind. Today, people spot the weak link and announce it to the world. Make sure your message accurately represents your business.

Social media forces you to be open, honest, and transparent. This fact makes many people nervous, but you really should embrace it and look at the upside. If you have a problem within your company, go and fix it. Stop trying to hide your warts. It is probably hurting your busines anyway, so fixing it can only help, right?

POTHOLES →

CAUTION! Avoid:

➤ Broadcasting not conversing

➤ Thinking you can control your marketing message

➤ Hiding sponsorships
This issue has become so important that the Federal Trade Commission (FTC) created rules that went into effect on December 1, 2009. You must disclose when you are being compensated, whether through payment or free product, and you must be truthful in your statements and speak from actual experience, rather than just using the sponsor's talking points.

Go to your audience, admit your shortcomings, and ask for feedback on how to improve. How's that for a novel concept? But here's the tricky part: you need to actually act on feedback and fix the problem. Once it has been fixed, communicate the change. I know it sounds scary, but it may be the best thing you have ever done.

Another point with transparency is that you should never try to hide the sponsorship of a spokesperson or blog. Someone will find out the truth, you will be exposed, and it will greatly damage your reputation.

➤ Right here, right now

Things move extremely fast in the world of social media and sometimes can snowball out of control. When launching a new initiative, you need to be prepared to keep your ears and eyes open for any issues. You can't launch something new on Friday night at 5 and then leave for the weekend. You may come in on Monday to a raging fire that has been simmering unattended all weekend.

Something similar happened to Motrin in September 2008. The company released ads that took a sarcastic view of the baby slings that moms wear. What Motrin was not prepared for was the backlash from moms on Twitter who were offended by the ads. It took Motrin awhile to respond, and by then it was a little too late for the apology to be accepted by the offended.

The Internet's evolution

Here is my favorite way to describe how the Internet has evolved over the years, and especially with the advent of social media. It all revolves around ice cream—specifically, the difference between the traditional ice cream store and the Good Humor truck.

For you to enjoy ice cream at an ice cream store, you need to put some level of effort into getting there. The store owners know that, and they also realize the amount of competition for your dollars. They offer competitive pricing and promote themselves through advertising and other marketing mediums. Their goal is to pull you into the store, which requires a certain level of effort on their part.

On the flipside, a Good Humor truck goes directly to where its audience is located—a neighborhood, park, pool, or beach. If the weather is nice and there are lots of children, then the Good Humor truck will likely be there too. The Good Humor drivers know exactly the best time to show up in these locations, usually after dinner or at afternoon snack time.

TALES FROM THE ROAD

Cowgirl Dirt
www.cowgirldirt.com

WHAT DO YOU KNOW NOW THAT YOU WISH YOU'D KNOWN BEFORE YOU DELVED INTO SOCIAL MEDIA?

When I first started, I wasn't as interactive and personal. I've become more personal and gotten to know more people. I wish I'd been more outgoing from the beginning. During the first month, I only had about 100 fans. Once I became more active, it really took off.

WHAT ADVICE WOULD YOU SHARE WITH OTHER BUSINESSES THAT ARE JUST GETTING STARTED WITH SOCIAL MEDIA?

Be yourself because you're dealing with real people. Social media is about building relationships, so don't be afraid to jump in.

EVALUATING WHERE YOU ARE NOW

To determine where your business is headed, we first have to step back and see where you've been. Let's look at what you've done in the past regarding marketing and then evaluate what's worked and what hasn't.

First, think about your business overall and what makes it stand out from the competition.

Your customer focus

Who is your customer base? Is it other businesses, consumers, government, non-profits? Your focus is often on more than one of these groups. Many business-to-consumer-based companies find opportunities to market to other businesses as well. The Kitchen Studio is a recreational cooking school that teaches tweens, teens, and adults how to cook, so its main focus is consumer. However, The Kitchen Studio also does private cooking classes and team-building events for companies, so it has a secondary focus on business-to-business.

Take a few minutes and think about whether your product or service has an audience beyond your current target market.

Competition

Think beyond your direct competition to include indirect competitors who perhaps are online or offer a substitute product or service to yours. Also remember that, depending on your product, you have to look beyond your local competition due to e-commerce.

Your USP (Unique Selling Proposition)

Simply stated, your USP is what makes your business different and therefore more valuable to your customers than competitive products or services. This difference—whether it's actual or perceived—should be used as part of your marketing. You may even want to consider incorporating your USP into your tagline.

Remember: Your USP is only valid if the target market actually sees it as a benefit to using your product or service over your competition. You should be able to prove your USP to the end user. Think of cable companies for a moment. Chances are they couldn't use customer service as their USP, because most of their customers would never believe it.

SWOT analysis

SWOT stands for Strengths, Weaknesses, Opportunities, and Threats. Each component is defined by whether it is something that helps or hurts you in reaching your business goals, as well as whether the influence is internal or external. An internal influence could be your staff, finances, or your product—all things over which you have some sense of control. An external influence could be the economy or weather, which are things you cannot control.

	HELPS YOU REACH YOUR GOALS	KEEPS YOU FROM REACHING YOUR GOALS
Internal	*Strengths*	*Weaknesses*
External	*Opportunities*	*Threats*

Strengths are internal influences that help you reach your goals and therefore are important to identify so you can use them to your advantage.

A weakness is also an internal influence, but it works against you in trying to reach your goals. Because the influence is internal, you have more control over fixing or eliminating the problem. The worst thing you can do is let your competitors use your weaknesses to their advantage.

Opportunities are external influences that can help you work toward your goals. Because these influences are external to the company, they are out of your control. They may be related to the economy, weather, technology, government, or culture. Your opportunities may be ever-changing due to these external factors.

Threats are external influences that can keep you from achieving your goals. Like opportunities, these threats are typically out of your control and can come from many different places. It's important to always keep potential sources of threats on your radar so you can take appropriate action when necessary.

To summarize, let me give you a scenario of a business and its SWOT analysis. Consider a restaurant that specializes in using only locally available and seasonal ingredients. Here is an example of what the restaurant's SWOT could look like:

➤ **Strength** – The owner of the restaurant has built successful restaurants before so he has the financial backing to succeed.

➤ **Weakness** – While the restaurant is financially secure, it has experienced a high rate of turnover, which is beginning to adversely affect customer service.

➤ **Opportunity** – Due to bloggers, recent documentaries, and recalls, the public has a lot of interest in where food comes from, so the idea of using locally-sourced food is a hit.

➤ **Threat** – A drought or other severe weather could adversely affect the supply of food, making it difficult for the restaurant to stick to its core values.

Now it's your turn. Think about your business and answer the following questions. This information will help you refocus your thinking onto your business so you can make effective decisions regarding your social media strategy.

Customer focus

....

What is your customer focus? _____

Business to consumer _____

Business to business _____

Business to government _____

Non-profit _____

Other _____

Competition

....

Direct competitors _____

_____

Indirect competitors _____

_____

Benefits over direct competitors _____

_____

Benefits over indirect competitors _____

_____

Unique Selling Proposition _____

_____

SWOT analysis

Strengths _____

_____

_____

Weaknesses _____

_____

_____

Opportunities _____

_____

_____

Threats _____

_____

_____

Now let's dig deeper into marketing and revisit the 4 P's—this time, from the perspective of your business.

Product

What are your products or services? _____

_____

_____

Do you offer them separately, as a bundle, or both? _____

_____

_____

Do you customize your product or service per customer? _____

_____

_____

Do you create your product or service or do you resell someone else's? _____

_____

_____

If you package your product, what is the packaging? _____

_____

_____

Do you offer any warranties or guarantees? _____

_____

What kind of support do you offer? _____

_____

_____

Do you have registered trademarks? _____

_____

_____

Price

How much do you charge for your product or service? _____

_____

_____

What kind of discounts do you offer? _____

_____

_____

Do you bundle products or services to create special pricing? _____

_____

_____

How does your pricing compare to your competition? _____

_____

_____

Is your pricing considered value or premium pricing? _____

Do you offer seasonal pricing? _____

_____

_____

Do you offer volume discounts? _____

_____

_____

Do you provide credit terms? _____

_____

_____

In what form(s) do you receive payment? (cash, check, credit cards) _____

_____

_____

Place (Distribution)

Do you sell your product/service directly to the consumer? _____

_____

_____

Do other companies sell your product? _____

_____

What is your market coverage (local, regional, national, international)? _____

_____

Do you have inventory? _____

_____

_____

What do you do with excess inventory items? _____

_____

_____

How do you deliver your product? _____

_____

_____

Promotion

....

Which of the following advertising tools do you use?

- ☐ Radio
- ☐ Television
- ☐ Print ads
- ☐ Direct mail
- ☐ Electronic (website, email newsletter)
- ☐ Word of mouth/referrals

Do you distribute press releases to the media? _____

Do you host events? _____

Do you attend trade shows? _____

Potential target audiences and messages

Knowing your audiences and the message you wish to deliver to them is the basis for everything we will do moving forward. It is important to understand all the different groups of your target audiences, their demographics (age, gender, etc.), their psychographics (their activities, attitudes, values), and where they go to get information on products and services that you provide.

Let's look first at who your target audiences may be and the types of messages you may want to deliver to them. Your final list will include some of these or even others not stated here.

➤ Prospects

If you want to sell your product or service, then you need people who want or need what you offer. You want them to know about your product or service so you and your business are "top of mind" when it's time for them to make a purchase.

A prospect typically reacts to third-party opinions much more than your message, so the more positive messages "out there" from your customers, the better. It helps to drown out the few negative comments that are bound to occur.

➤ Customers

A current customer can be your greatest asset, especially if he or she is a very happy customer. These satisfied customers become both repeat customers and brand ambassadors for you and your brand. Social media gives these brand ambassadors the ability to show their allegiance by "liking" you, for example, on Facebook or following your Twitter updates or your blog. It also gives your fans the ability to share their love for your brand with others. Customers aren't easy to come by; once you have them, don't leave them in the cold. Nurture your customer relationships every chance you have.

➤ Media

This audience is often overlooked unless you consistently do public relations for your company. The landscape for media has also changed in that you now need to consider bloggers as part of your outreach programs. Show that you are a subject-matter expert, and the media will seek you out as a source. Make it easy for them to learn the latest news about your business. To be effective you have to deliver a very personal message to each media representative, showing that you have taken the time to understand his or her work.

➤ Partners

A partner is someone who is not an employee of your company but works hand in hand with you as a third party. Examples include resellers, wholesalers, franchisees, or sub-contractors. They help you run your business in one way or another, and you rely on them as though they were employees. They are a trusted party.

You need to communicate with this group differently than a customer. They need insider information that will make them more effective in working with you. This group often needs the information before you release it to the public. For this reason, this information is often found protected with passwords or other layers of security.

The types of messages you may want to deliver to this group are marketing materials, product specifications and launch information, support issues, and pricing. This group is often overlooked and shouldn't be; they are as important to your success as customers.

➤ Investors

Investors have some type of investment in your organization, whether it is time, money, or some other resource. This group often includes shareholders and board members. They want to understand your mission to ensure it is still in line with their own beliefs but also so they can be effective in spreading the word about your business.

This group can be a major asset as they will go out and inform their networks about you and your product or service. Provide them with the message and tools that make it easier to share your information.

➤ Internal

Current employees have a vested interest in the success of your company. The better you do, the better they do.

The messages you share with employees should go beyond product knowledge and marketing information, which of course is important in helping them to evangelize your company. They also need information that makes them feel better about their jobs. You need to communicate with them regarding human resources issues, such as job openings, benefit changes, and policy issues. You can also let them know about company events, sales goals, and so on.

➤ Potential employees

Beyond current employees, you should reach out to potential employees. Finding the best and the brightest can be quite a competitive search. You want to put your best foot forward.

In addition to open positions and information on your benefits package, you want to give recruits a behind-the-scenes look. Potential employees want to know what the company's culture is as much as the pay scale. Give them a feel for a day-in-the-life of your company.

➤ Community

A topic that has become much more important recently is what a company does with respect to social responsibility. Does the company support local and national causes? What about employees? How are you giving back and making a difference?

Even if you don't sell directly to customers where your business is located, it is still important to communicate with residents on how you give back to the community.

Your turn

Now it is time for you to list up to four audiences you are currently targeting, along with the message you are trying to deliver to each one:

Audience 1 _____

Message _____

_____

Audience 2 _____

Message _____

_____

Audience 3 _____

Message _____

_____

Audience 4 _____

Message _____

_____

The information you have put together in this chapter will be the basis for your social media strategy as we move forward.

TALES FROM THE ROAD

Golden Path Alchemy
www.goldenpathalchemy.com

BIGGEST CHALLENGE?

Time. All of these things take time—time to write blogs, updates, etc.

K9 Confections
www.k9confections.com

WHAT WAS YOUR BIGGEST FEAR BEFORE STARTING WITH SOCIAL MEDIA – AND WAS THE FEAR WARRANTED?

My fear was that no one would want to read what was being written. Fortunately, that fear never showed its head. We have been pleasantly surprised with the interest it has generated.

TAKING INVENTORY OF YOUR CURRENT TOOLS

Remember that social media does not live on its own outside your marketing plan. It needs to be integrated in order to be effective. For this reason, we will now look at your current marketing activities and how we can integrate social media into the mix.

To get started, let's list the marketing tools you use now. I've included a few, but you will probably need to add other items that you've used in the past or are currently using as part of your promotional mix.

For each item, provide more details such as when and how often it is used, the target audience, the message or call to action, and any results:

Current marketing tools

Website _____

_____

_____

Banner ads on other websites _____

_____

_____

Text-based ads (Google AdWords) _____

_____

_____

Email newsletter _____

_____

_____

Point of Purchase (POP) display _____

_____

_____

Trials or demonstrations of your product/service

    Online _____

    In person _____

Presentations

    Webinars _____

    In person _____

Direct mail _____

_____

_____

Print advertising _____

_____

_____

Exhibits

  Trade shows _____

  Conferences _____

Sponsorships _____

_____

_____

Radio _____

_____

_____

Television _____

_____

_____

Other _____

_____

_____

From the current marketing tools you just listed, indicate which three are the:

Most effective:

1. _____

2. _____

3. _____

Least effective:

1. _____

2. _____

3. _____

You only have so many hours in the day and only so much money to allocate, so adding social media to your list may look nearly impossible. But consider this: If you stop using the three least effective marketing tools you listed and shift that time to your social media initiatives, you don't have to find more time in the day.

Think about it. Could you cut any of the items from the least effective list to devote resources (time and money) to social media? If so, which one(s)? About how many hours in a week would that free up? _____

_____

_____

Integrate what is working

Let's look again at your list of the most effective marketing tools you are using and identify opportunities to integrate your existing marketing with social media.

Integration allows you to extend your message through new mediums and tools. These days, you are more likely to see a Facebook address at the end of television commercials than a website address. I love the idea of extending an ad to YouTube for behind-the-scenes or additional footage, such as what Toyota did with the Sienna minivan, aka the Swagger wagon.

Another great example of integration is marrying your blog with your email newsletter. Add links to your blog within the body of your newsletter because each tool may have a different audience.

You've heard me say it before, and I will say it again: social media does not stand on its own. It needs to be leveraged throughout your business to extend your message to the correct audience.

Make what you have work

I am a big fan of reusing marketing materials whenever possible. Let's face it: each one takes a lot of time and money to put together. You should get as much use as possible out of them. As you evaluate any marketing tool, including social media, remember to ask yourself if it will effectively reach your target audience with your desired message.

To get you thinking about the resources you may already have in-house, I have created a list of 10 items that I know a lot of companies have sitting around in a closet somewhere.

➤ Press kit

As part of my first job out of college, I was responsible for assembling the press kits. I cannot even begin to count how many paper jams I cleared or how many paper cuts I nursed. I had a love/hate relationship with press kits. While many companies have abandoned the printed press kit in the fancy folder, it is still probably a pdf tucked away somewhere in the news section of the website. To make your press kit more "social," consider creating a social media newsroom. Pull pieces from the kit—for example, company history, owner's bio, latest news, etc.—and let them stand on their own in the newsroom. In this way, you can communicate your company's news, successes, and background with both the press and the public.

➤ White papers

Technology companies are known for producing a lot of white papers. While these documents have their place, the information contained within can be repurposed and reformatted into e-books and podcasts. E-books tend to be more user-friendly because they have more pictures and the information is laid out in an easy-to-read format. Another option is to transform your white paper info into a podcast, which allows your audience to take the information on the road with them.

➤ Demonstrations

Do you have a product that can be demonstrated and captured as a screencast? What about taking a video of your product or service being used? A video of how to play a game would go a long way to help customers through the decision-making process. Place this video on your site, blog, or other video-sharing sites. Videos and screencasts help visitors see your product in action without using it themselves.

➤ Promotional products

Companies that go to trade shows always have extra promotional products lying around gathering dust until the next show. Why not have some fun and run a trivia contest on Twitter and give away extra products to followers? Provide an incentive to engage with you and your company through social networks and give your

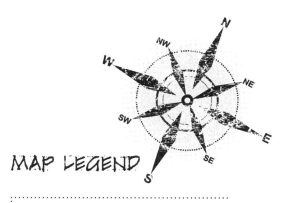

MAP LEGEND

WHITE PAPER is a document that addresses a problem and how to solve it and is used as a marketing tool, meaning that the solution to the problem usually involves the use of the company's product or service.

PODCAST is a series of audio or video files produced on a regular basis and downloaded via subscription.

SCREENCAST is a recording of activity that is takes place on your computer screen. These are often narrated and used to show the viewer how to do something on a website or with a computer program.

followers a little token of your appreciation. If nothing else, you'll clear out that closet!

➤ Presentation slides

Post presentations on SlideShare, which is a repository for presentations that visitors can view and comment upon. Depending on the presentation, you could also convert it to an audio or video podcast to showcase the information in different ways.

➤ Webinars

Transform audio info into a podcast that can stand on its own. You can also consider posting these webinars to video-sharing sites. Different members of your audience consume media in different ways, so being able to connect with them in a variety of mediums is to your advantage.

➤ Case studies

Use case studies as a foundation for blog posts on your corporate blog. See if you can work with your clients to do interviews and put that interview on video for use on your site, blog, and video-sharing sites. I personally love the idea of video testimonials. It does not have to be a totally scripted, produced video; it can be a video camera set up on a tripod and two people talking. You can even encourage other customers to record their own testimonials and upload them to your video-sharing page or fan page.

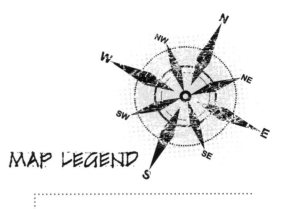

MAP LEGEND

SLIDESHARE is a website used for storing and sharing presentations, mostly those created in PowerPoint.
www.slideshare.net

WEBINAR is the use of web-based conferencing to conduct a meeting or presentation to a group of people in different locations via the Internet.

➤ Videos

Maybe you have videos of someone in your company giving a speech to an audience. Consider posting this to video-sharing sites, such as YouTube, or providing it for download on your website. Check through those video archives and see what gems you may be able to use. Be sure to think twice before uploading that video of the holiday party in 1999.

➤ Frequently Asked Questions (FAQs)

If you have a series of questions that are frequently asked by clients and prospects, then consider creating blog posts using this information. Some companies don't have a public set of FAQs, but on a daily basis they answer the same questions via phone and email. Take the burden off your staff and put these items on a blog where people can search for them or you can link to in future emails.

➤ Staff

Your staff may be an untapped resource when it comes to social media. They may already interact on social networks or have a passion to blog. Talk to your staff and see if they are interested in engaging your clients through social media. Let them become your evangelists and community managers. You may be surprised at the results. Be sure to set up some company guidelines with respect to the use of social media.

Now look again at your list of current marketing tools and see if there is any content you can recycle to use in social media. For example, whenever you educate someone about your product or industry on a one-on-one basis through email or discussion, you have content for a blog post. If you have a list of Frequently Asked Questions (FAQs), you have blog content. If you have historical information such as pictures or videos, you have fun information to share online and show your organization's personality. If you have inventory, you could have giveaway items to run a simple and effective contest.

List some content you can recycle in your social media efforts:

1. _____

_____

_____

2. _____

_____

_____

3. _____

_____

_____

4. _____

_____

_____

5. _____

_____

_____

POTHOLES ➤

CAUTION! Avoid:

➤ Not integrating social media into your complete marketing plan.

We have looked at your past and present marketing efforts, and in the next chapter we will start planning your future strategies. I hope you have been writing down your thoughts, because you are going to need to reference them in the upcoming chapters.

TALES FROM THE ROAD

Royal Country Clubs
www.golfatroyal.com

BIGGEST SUCCESS?

Our membership, both young and old, are on Facebook and Twitter. Allowing different age groups to become a part of our Facebook page has been great. We are able to market last-minute specials, rain delays, and course closures instantly. Being from Chicago, the weather changes instantly and our social media tools allow us to keep our membership updated.

WHAT ADVICE WOULD YOU SHARE WITH OTHER BUSINESSES THAT ARE JUST GETTING STARTED WITH SOCIAL MEDIA?

Always monitor who is following you or who your fans are. Respond to their questions or their complaints. Don't be afraid of starting social media because people may complain; the best part about it is that it allows you a voice. It allows other people to see your personality and how you react to problems.

Turn the page for more TALES FROM THE ROAD ➤➤

The Pintley Company
www.pintley.com

BIGGEST SUCCESS?

We used Twitter to land a big PR success with Thrillist.com. Thrillist's recent article brought thousands of visitors to Pintley with a 33 percent conversion rate.

WHAT ADVICE WOULD YOU SHARE WITH OTHER BUSINESSES THAT ARE JUST GETTING STARTED WITH SOCIAL MEDIA?

Have a social media plan. It's not enough to create a Twitter and Facebook account and expect people to come to you. You need to engage them in an active, meaningful way. Create valuable content, not spam. Just like with the rest of your business, if you provide value, you'll do well; if you don't, you'll fail.

StormSister Spatique
www.stormsister.biz

BIGGEST SUCCESS?

Finding a site that lets me post to all networks. Being "out there" has gotten me connected with many beauty editors and journalists. This has been very beneficial as I build my brand and get into product development.

WHAT ADVICE WOULD YOU SHARE WITH OTHER BUSINESSES THAT ARE JUST GETTING STARTED WITH SOCIAL MEDIA?

You must make it mandatory. It is so important to connect with clients on this level. You are foolish not to do it. Learn it.

PLANNING WHERE YOU WANT TO GO

Let's move forward and look at the opportunities that social media offers your organization.

Like anything in business, social media is most effective when you set goals to determine what you want to get out of the effort you invest. Sometimes the success or failure of these goals can be measured, and at other times it is more subjective.

Here are some of the main goals that social media can help you achieve. Feel free to add your own to the list:

- Increase sales
- Increase traffic
- Boost awareness
- Establish thought leadership
- Grow your connections and networking
- Improve customer service
- Connect with the media
- Promote events
- Encourage customer input/feedback
- Generate word of mouth
- Reward customer loyalty

- Clear out inventory
- Educate and inform

Let's dive in and explore each one of these in more detail.

Increase sales

Increasing your sales is really the main goal of all your marketing, right? Not everything you do in social media will have this result, but everything should have an indirect effect or it isn't worth pursuing.

StormSister Spatique sells products for men, women, and children, including aromatherapy, skin care, and bath and body products. StormSister uses Twitter, Facebook, and its blog to market directly to consumers. The company has gained many new clients as a result of its social media activity.

Nomie Baby, manufacturer of car seat covers, has been found by retailers on Twitter who want to carry the company's products, showing that social media doesn't just work with the end user.

Increase traffic

Social media can help you increase traffic to your online presence and/or to your actual office or store. This goal often feeds into the goal of increased sales as well. The increase in traffic allows you to introduce your company and product to your audiences and convert them into customers. In addition, you may want to increase repeat traffic and not just new traffic.

Help My Resume is a resume rewriting service aimed at helping the unemployed find work. Through the creation and execution of its social media strategy, the company increased traffic to its website by 276.3 percent, which in turn helped to grow their customer base by 37.2 percent.

Sometimes an increase in website traffic can lead to more than just sales. A website dedicated to helping its users manage their retirement accounts, eRollover, was able to increase traffic to its site, which was instrumental in securing eRollover's first round of business funding.

Boost awareness

Brand awareness and staying top of mind with your audience is a very important goal. When the consumer finally has a need for your product or service and considers your business at that time, then you will have succeeded in building awareness.

New York Guest provides services for easier travel and meeting planning in New York City. By growing its Facebook page to 10,000 users, New York Guest is able to keep this audience aware of its services even when Facebook users are not planning a trip to the Big Apple.

Establish thought leadership

Thought leadership is an important goal but a little harder to measure. To achieve thought leadership, you must position yourself and your company as experts. You know you are the expert and so do your customers, but your prospects may not—at least not yet. Providing information about your industry and your product helps differentiate you from your competition.

The owner of InvisibleShoe.com, Steven Sashen, is hands-on with his social media efforts. From involvement in discussion groups to videos demonstrating his barefoot running shoe, he has created thought leadership with his audience. When he goes to barefoot running events, he is often recognized as the "guy in the videos," which buys him instant credibility.

Grow your connections and networking

I consider the best part of social media to be the connections you can make online and then extend and strengthen in real life. Another great thing about networking via social media is that it knows no time or geographical barriers. You can engage with people anywhere and at times that work best for your schedule, even if you are thousands of miles away.

In addition to thought leadership, networking is one of my personal goals with social media. I especially like to use Twitter for connecting with people in the area and then meeting them for coffee or lunch. It allows me to expand my network and meet potential partners as well as clients.

Improve customer service

Beyond marketing, social media helps companies improve customer service. Whether it is listening for people having problems or people coming directly to you for help, social media facilitates the conversation easily and effectively.

Beacon Adhesives, a manufacturer of glue for many different industries and uses, has found social media effective for addressing customer service issues. Through monitoring, Beacon can listen for complaints about its products. The company can reach out quickly to remedy the problem, which is effective in building positive word of mouth and happy customers.

Connect with the media

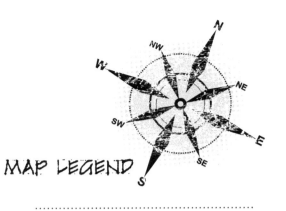

For some businesses, media relations is an important marketing goal. Using social media tools can be a very effective way to keep the media informed of your activities. In addition to the press, there are bloggers in every industry with whom you can build relationships.

Pintley.com makes personalized beer recommendations, and through the use of Twitter was able to land an article on Thrillist.com. The article brought thousands of visitors to Pintley's website with a 33 percent conversion rate of turning them into members.

Promote events

Inviting people to events and allowing them to RSVP online and through social media tools can help increase attendee numbers. Whether you're planning a fundraising event, educational seminar, or just something fun, social media allows people to interact with you before, during, and after the event.

AtNetPlus, Inc. provides technology services to small businesses and has found promoting education events through LinkedIn to be very successful. The company can connect with other professionals who are interested in the traning AtNetPlus provides.

MAP LEGEND

LINKEDIN is a social network focused mainly on connecting professionals with each other. Its main purpose is professional networking.
www.linkedin.com

Encourage customer input/feedback

Take advantage of the conversational nature of social media and have your own personal focus group. Marketing research and focus groups can be cost-prohibitive to small businesses, but social media offers a more casual and inexpensive approach. Ask your audience what they like and don't like.

The owners of my favorite toy store, Dancing Bear Toys and Gifts (mentioned in Chapter 2), will often post a product they are thinking about adding to their inventory on their Facebook page to gather opinions. They are able to determine simply and effectively whether there will be a market for this product.

Generate word of mouth

Your raving fans are among your best assets, so let them get out there and spread the word on your behalf. People are almost always more willing to believe a third-party source rather than the company. Provide tools that allow your fans to spread the word.

Brewster House Bed and Breakfast in Freeport, Maine, has been effective in using social media to make connections, which have led to positive word of mouth, referrals, and recommendations from this loyal audience. By keeping people informed and engaged, Brewster House stays "top of mind" when quality accomodations are needed.

Reward customer loyalty

It's no secret that it is less expensive to keep a customer happy than to acquire a new one. Keep those customers happy with special offers and promotions. Also, include customers in the process by asking for feedback and—above all else—make it fun.

Holistic, handmade, herbal skin care company Golden Path Alchemy offers coupons via social networks. Golden Path uses specific codes for each network, so the company can track which networks are most successful.

Clear out inventory

Maybe you have a few extra products at the end of a selling season. Create a special promotion for your audience that will help to clear the extra inventory and generate "buzz" for your business at the same time.

As I mentioned in Chapter 2, Dell Computers uses Twitter to promote items in their Outlet Store. Since the Twitter account was launched, Dell has sold more than $6 million of product via this account.

Educate

Similar to thought leadership, educating your audience can elevate you to expert status. Beyond that, educating customers on proper use of your product, for example, may also decrease support costs. Maybe there are alternative uses for your product that you can also share. The possibilities are endless.

Elena Adams Designs sells handcrafted jewelry, and the owner has used social media to educate her audience using videos. These videos take the viewer behind-the-scenes to see the level of work that goes into the creation of her jewelry.

There are other goals that may be more specific to your business so be sure to include those as we move forward. You may have multiple goals for each audience as well. There really is no right or wrong way to define goals. The only wrong answer is NOT defining any goals. Without goals, you won't know if your efforts are successful.

Take another look at your target audience list that you put together in the last chapter. Now select the three audiences you want to focus on with regard to social media. You can go back and add more at a later date, but let's start with something manageable.

In addition to the audience name, write down the message you want to deliver to that specific audience and the goal. Review the goals discussed in this chapter and use one of those or add your own. It is fine to have two goals for each audience, but keep it to one overall message.

Audience 1 _____

Message _____

_____

Goal _____

_____

Audience 2 _____

Message _____

_____

Goal _____

_____

Audience 3 _____

Message _____

_____

Goal _____

_____

Audience 4 _____

Message _____

_____

Goal _____

_____

Before we go any further, I want you to really understand what it means to start engaging people in social media. Social media can be a big step for people and companies because it requires two-way conversations, not just pushing out a promotion.

I am not trying to frighten you away from social media, but I want you to spend a few minutes on a reality check. Ask yourself:

➤ Am I ready for feedback, both good and bad?

Don't get me wrong—most feedback will be positive unless you have some underlying problem within your organization or negative sentiment in the marketplace. The key is to be prepared to handle the negative feedback. Don't worry, Chapter 8 will get you prepared.

➤ Am I willing to give more than I receive?

In social media, it is not all about you. You must be willing to help others and even promote others. I'm not saying you go out there and promote your competition, but if someone you follow has something worth sharing, be sure to pass it on. The giving will be returned in kind and will be much more beneficial to you.

➤ Am I ready to let my community own my message?

For years, marketers have felt that they controlled the message they broadcast to the masses—even though we know people have created not-so-flattering nicknames for companies and formed their own opinions through word of mouth and experience.

Social media puts your community in control of your message once you have communicated it. Many of your loyal customers will be happy to rave to their networks about how much they enjoy your company and product.

➤ Am I committed to not abandoning my accounts because I don't see immediate results?

Social media success rarely happens overnight. It takes some time to build and nurture your community. By setting goals, you will be more inclined to push on and gain that success. I see so many accounts that have three posts and then are abandoned. Get out there and connect—and keep connecting.

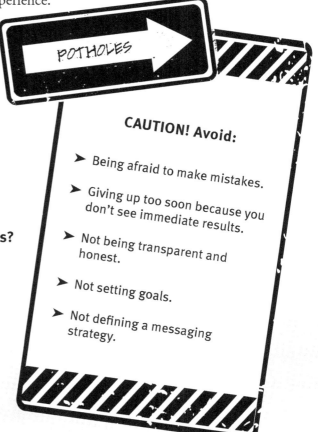

POTHOLES

CAUTION! Avoid:

➤ Being afraid to make mistakes.

➤ Giving up too soon because you don't see immediate results.

➤ Not being transparent and honest.

➤ Not setting goals.

➤ Not defining a messaging strategy.

➤ Am I ready to be open, honest, and transparent?

I don't mean giving up the keys to the castle, but you need to be open and honest about your operations. If people even think you are lying or trying to hide something, they will search out the truth and expose you. Let's face it—lying is hard because you have to remember what the lie is. Just stay honest and you'll be fine.

➤ Am I ready to show the human side and personality of my business?

People want to know more about the people who make a company tick. Again, for privacy's sake, you don't want to tell them everything, but you want them to get a sense of the personalities behind the logo. Business is about relationships, and you want to connect on a human level.

➤ Am I ready to experiment and make mistakes?

Social media is still a relatively new medium for marketing. Everyone makes mistakes, and you will, too. The key is to be willing to try something new and different. If it is a success, great. If it fails, move on. Also, know that you may make a mistake that requires an apology. When that happens, say you are sorry and try to not repeat that behavior.

➤ Am I ready to engage?

I've said it before and I will say it again, social media is about two-way conversations. The tools and sites used for these conversations will change and evolve, but the conversation is here to stay.

Don't be afraid to reach out and say hi or offer help. That's exactly why people use social media—to connect with other people. People will seek you out as well, so make sure you respond.

➤ Am I ready to have fun?

Social media should be fun. It's not about the technology; it truly is about the conversations and connections. Don't be about business all the time. Share fun links, ask fun questions, or jump into conversations that may not be relevant to your company. You never know where that conversation may lead you.

If you answered "yes" to the previous questions, then you are ready to add social media to your marketing mix. You have selected your audiences, your messages, and goals. Now let's lay some groundwork so you can be properly prepared for your social media journey.

TALES FROM THE ROAD

Simplicity Mastered
www.simplicitymastered.com

WHAT ADVICE WOULD YOU SHARE WITH OTHER BUSINESSES THAT ARE JUST GETTING STARTED WITH SOCIAL MEDIA?

➤ Know your social media objective (i.e. increase traffic, increase clients, brand exposure, share expertise, etc.).

➤ Have a simple plan (one page explaining your method of operation and management).

➤ Track, Track, Track... Monitor, Monitor, Monitor.

➤ Be mindful of your brand. Everything you post is up for grabs and critique.

➤ Time management.

WHAT WAS YOUR BIGGEST FEAR BEFORE STARTING WITH SOCIAL MEDIA - AND WAS THE FEAR WARRANTED?

Being exposed or too accessible. Totally unfounded. In fact, the exposure and accessibility worked in my favor.

SETTING UP YOUR LISTENING POST

Social media is about the conversations that take place online every day about brands, people, products, and industries. If you are not listening to these conversations, you are missing opportunities to engage with your different target audiences. These conversations can be both positive and negative, but if you are not aware of them, then you risk losing valuable opportunities to learn and engage. Rest assured that your competitors are listening, and they are using the information to their advantage.

Sales funnel

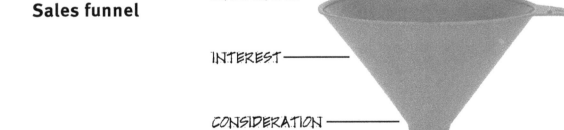

Let's think about the traditional sales funnel that people go through during the purchasing process. When people determine they have a need, they begin in the awareness/interest stage, move through consideration of products and brands, and finally complete an action, such as making a purchase.

Customer megaphone

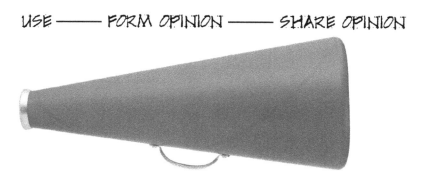

Once a purchase has been made or a similar action has been taken, consumers transition into what I call the Customer Megaphone. They use the product, decide whether they like it or not and why, and then they most likely share their opinion of the product or service. In the past, this sharing of opinion was limited to a small network of people—typically family members, co-workers, and social circles. Now that social media is in the picture, the sharing network has expanded dramatically.

The big picture

To better illustrate my point, I'd like to introduce my "fish of influence" —a more visually appealing combination of the sales funnel and the customer megaphone. Like the sales funnel, you follow the purchasing process from the bottom fin up the back of the fish to where the action takes place. This action is usually a purchase but could be whatever action you are trying to elicit from the consumer.

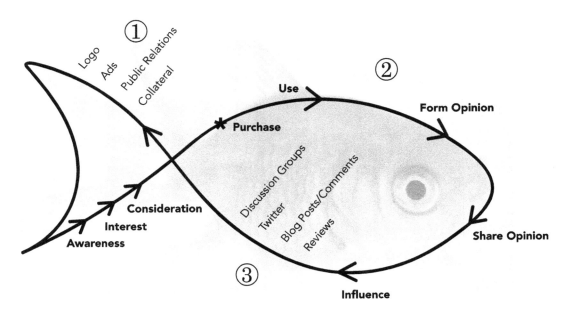

copyright 2009,
VillageWorks Communications, Inc.

① On the top fin you see traditional marketing materials that aid the consumer during the purchase cycle, namely your logo, advertisements, public relations, and other marketing collateral. In the past, these were the items that most influenced the consumer.

② As we continue on the back of the fish, after the action takes place, we move into the elements of the megaphone: use, form opinion, and share opinion. Now we see how social media completely changes the game.

③ In the world of social media, people share their opinions beyond their personal network and in much more public areas than ever before—such as online reviews, blog posts and comments, social networks, and discussion groups. This sharing of opinions is becoming increasingly more influential and should not be ignored by you or your company. This influence can have much more impact on repeat and prospective customers' purchasing cycles than any marketing materials you produce. It's important to use these influences to your advantage by celebrating the champions and engaging the detractors.

The goal then becomes finding these influencers. Before you put the pedal to the metal on your social media journey, you need to spend some time listening—and learning.

Why listen?

➤ Know where your audience is. There's no need to make random guesses about where to start your social media efforts. You can find out exactly where you need to be.

➤ Know what your audience is saying. You can learn what types of words consumers use to describe your product, your company, and your industry. Maybe you call it a note book computer, but your audience calls it a laptop. You will want to adjust your lan guage accordingly. Doing so will help you shape your message both online and off.

➤ Use your resources wisely. The information you glean by listening leads to a smarter use of both your time and money.

➤ Manage your reputation. Find out where you stand with your audience in terms of positive, negative, or neutral comments. Maybe there are no discussions at all. Knowing this information can help you determine your initial goals. (We'll come back to this topic later.)

➤ Get smart about the competition. While you're learning about yourself and your business, you can also learn the same things about your competition. Who's saying what about your competitors? Are they seen in a negative or positive light? Are there common questions regarding their product that might relate to your product? If so, maybe you need to adjust your marketing efforts accordingly.

Selecting keywords

So how do you become an effective listener? You set up a listening post to eavesdrop on the online conversations and learn to engage at the appropriate times. Even before you select the best monitoring tools for your listening post, you need to determine what you want to "hear." Selecting the right keywords to search for can make or break your monitoring. If you search for too general of terms, you will get more information than you can sort through. Choose keywords that are too specific, and you may miss conversations.

My advice is to start with a large list, do a little searching, and then refine your list from there.

To begin, organize all the keywords you can think of into the following categories:

Your company name _____

_____

_____

Executive/owner name(s) _____

_____

_____

Product or service name(s) _____

_____

_____

Web address (if different than company name) _____

_____

Competitor company name(s) _____

_____

_____

Competitor product/service name(s) _____

_____

_____

Competitor executives _____

_____

_____

Competitor web address (if different than company name) _____

_____

_____

Industry-specific keywords _____

_____

_____

_____

Revise your list

The biggest problem you may encounter with your keywords is that they may be too general, particularly when it comes to names of companies or products and services. For example, Apple as a company name is too general and needs to be linked with another keyword, such as computers, iPhone, iPod, etc., to get the desired result. You may need to add words to create a phrase or use AND/OR as part of your searches. The more specific your searches, the more accurate your results.

To fine-tune your keywords, do a simple Google search on your keyword and look at the results. Did you get the results you wanted? If not, add keywords that complement your initial keyword until you begin to see the results you want.

Some of this process is trial and error, but do as much legwork in the beginning so you are not constantly revising keywords in your listening post. Frequent changes will affect your results if the monitoring tool does not allow you to search archives for mentions made before today's date.

Look at your original list again and refine it with any complementary words to be included in the search phrase:

Your company name _____

_____

_____

Executive/owner name(s) _____

_____

_____

Product or service name(s) _____

_____

_____

Web address (if different than company name) _____

_____

Competitor company name(s) _____

_____

_____

Competitor product/service name(s) _____

_____

_____

Competitor executives _____

_____

_____

Competitor web address (if different than company name) _____

_____

_____

Industry-specific keywords _____

_____

_____

Monitoring tools

Depending on the monitoring tools you use, you may be able to set up filters to eliminate some sources that aren't relevant to what you want to track. For example, while you want mentions of your web address by other people, you do not want to see mentions from content on your own website. You want to filter out the results that come from your website as a source.

Here is a list of things to add to the filter of your monitoring tool, if applicable:

- Your website URL

- Your blog URL

- Any URL associated with your service if it is a hosted service

- Any URL associated with your social media sites, such as Twitter, YouTube, Flickr, etc.

Free versus paid monitoring tools

There are many options available to you, and I'm not going to make a judgment call about which is better. Here are a few points to consider:

The fact that the <u>free tools</u> are free is their main advantage. Free tools are great for small businesses and well suited for companies and organizations that are starting out with social media and need their first listening post.

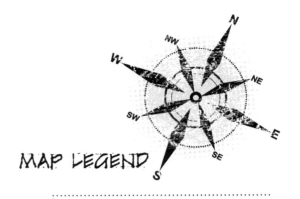

MAP LEGEND

FREE TOOLS
- Google Alerts
- Twitter search
- FriendDeck
- BoardTracker

PAID MONITORING TOOLS
- Trackur
- SM2
- Radian6

GOOGLE SEARCH HINTS
- Exact phrase use quotes: "social media"

- Exclude keywords: social media –tools

- Search specific to one site "social media" site: **www.mashable.com**

- Similar words: "social media" ~marketing

- This OR that: social media OR marketing

To accompany their typically high price tags, <u>paid monitoring tools</u> do have some important advantages:

- Can search on historical data, which can be very useful. Many of these tools allow you to search through their past stores of data to find your keywords. This feature is particularly helpful in creating benchmarks.

- Provide automatic reports and charts of mentions

- Allow you to set up filters to eliminate sources you don't want to track

- Require less time to set up

- Typically have more thorough results because they are searching many more sources

If you are just starting out, the free services will work well for you, but as time goes on you may find it necessary to step up to one of the paid services. Armed with your keywords and the tools for monitoring, you are ready to set up your listening post.

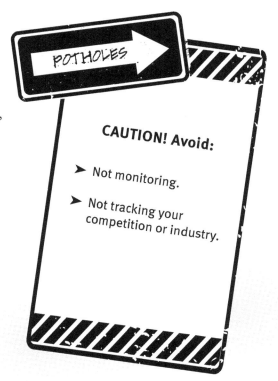

POTHOLES

CAUTION! Avoid:

➤ Not monitoring.

➤ Not tracking your competition or industry.

 TALES FROM THE ROAD

InvisibleShoe.com
www.invisibleshoe.com

BIGGEST SUCCESS?

Our entire promotion has been through social media and search engine marketing. In less than three months we went from inception to full-time business. Our participation on the forums results in great credibility (especially after I posted my times in the 100m and people saw that I wasn't just a running shoe maker, but also a nationally ranked sprinter). Our videos have been embedded in lots of sites... I go to barefoot running events and people get extremely excited to see me live ("OH MY GOD... you're that guy in the videos!").

Beacon Adhesives
www.beaconadhesives.com

BIGGEST SUCCESS?

Our biggest success is in responding to discussions about our products on the Internet. We are able, using search terms, to find content and enter into a discussion as the "voice" of our product, rather than waiting for people to call us on our 800 number to ask questions or complain. We can turn a negative experience into a positive for the consumer, who will then re-post his/her interaction with our company.

AtNetPlus, Inc.
www.atnetplus.com

BIGGEST SUCCESS?

LinkedIn has allowed us to reach more professionals for promoting events that we host. The number of attendees has increased dramatically due to our activity on LinkedIn.

YOU'RE LISTENING. NOW WHAT?

Great! Now you are monitoring the Internet for your keywords, but you're probably wondering what to do with all the data you collect. The information you gather provides:

- A benchmark by which to compare all future campaigns
- Knowledge about where your target audiences spend their time—and what they're talking about
- Insight into how your audience feels about you and your product
- Competitive intelligence regarding what others say about the competition, where they say it, and how they feel about it

What to track

Here's what you should be tracking while you are monitoring:

- Number of valid mentions by day and/or week
- Source of mentions
- Number of good mentions
- Number of bad mentions
- Number of neutral mentions

- Type of mention
- Department of the company in the mention (sales, human resources, customer service, etc.)

Let's dig into each one for more detail.

➤ Number of mentions total and by keyword

You should review mentions on a daily basis to make sure you aren't missing anything that needs to be addressed. You should also track mentions on a weekly basis to keep an eye on trends. Be sure to track mentions by keyword so you can see what is being discussed the most.

What you learn: Volume of mentions for your keywords, specifically your company versus your competitors.

You will also learn if a spike in mentions occurred and what may have caused that spike. Some contributing factors could be:

- Product launch
- Press release
- Coverage by a blog
- Competitive announcement
- A problem that sparked a firestorm

Why important: This original number becomes a baseline comparison for future campaigns. The hope is that the number of mentions will increase as you engage your audience. Of course, positive mentions would be a plus, and we'll discuss that soon.

➤ Source of mentions

What you learn: Where your audience is. This information is one of the biggest advantages of monitoring. Now you can put that information to work for you.

More specifically you will also learn who the influencers are in your industry. While you don't need to track every source, you do want to look for patterns and for influential sources who are authorities in your industry.

Why important: You can discover sites that you didn't know existed, find out where your audience spends time, and become an active member in that community.

You can also start engaging with any influential bloggers you discover by leaving comments on posts—and not just the posts in which he or she mentions you. Become a voice and resource to the community. Remember—no blatant selling. Provide expertise and thought leadership.

➤ High number of positive mentions

The people praising or complimenting you or your business can be an asset to your community. It is to your advantage to identify these individuals and leverage their enthusiasm.

What you learn: Your community has an overall positive sentiment about your company and product.

Why important: As you start or continue with your social media efforts, you know you have a supportive and perhaps even enthusiastic community. Invite them to join you (if they haven't already) wherever your social media efforts are taking place. Allow them to evangelize for you and make it easy for them to do so by providing sneak peeks, special offers, insider news, etc.

➤ High number of neutral mentions

What you learn: When the mentions that you track are neither overly positive or negative in nature, we consider them neutral. These are usually the largest quantity of mentions you will have—unless you have a very polarizing product or service. Most neutral mentions are from news or press releases about you. They have more to do with fact than opinion.

Why important: If you are starting out in social media, then you know you have nothing to address with regard to negativity, but you also may not have any enthusiastic champions to leverage either. People may like your company and/or product, but they are not passionate. Through engagement, it is possible to turn them into raving fans.

If you have been using social media for awhile and things are still pretty neutral, don't panic. Not every organization's community is as enthusiastic as Apple's, for example. Don't give up. Continue to nurture relationships and give your target audiences something to be excited about.

➤ High number of negative mentions

Negative mentions come in many different forms, with some being relevant and others not. Negative mentions can be complaints about your product or service that need to be addressed. Unfortunately they can also be from individuals I refer to as Trolls. We'll discuss how to handle this group of people in the next chapter.

Your biggest goal with negative mentions is to get to the root of the person's issue and try to remedy the problem as soon as possible. Often when you are able to remedy a situation, that person will become a very loyal champion of your cause.

What you learn: For one reason or another, people have a negative sentiment about your company and your products.

Why important: You need to get to the root of the negative sentiment. Is it an issue that can be fixed? If yes, fix it. If not, then you'd better be able to provide a solid explanation.

If the issue can be fixed, ask for feedback from those who have complained about how to make it better. Be sure to actually fix the problem and not just "spin" the situation. If you get caught lying about the fix, you will have a much worse problem on your hands.

Once the issue has been resolved, announce it and invite feedback on the fix.

➤ Type of mentions

Where you find the mention is as important as the source. Is it Twitter, a blog post, blog comment, news site, Facebook, etc?

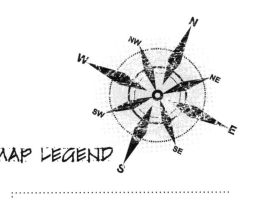

MAP LEGEND

RETWEET takes place on Twitter. A user passes along someone else's tweet, usually noted by a "RT" (for retweet) in the tweet.

What you learn: This information lets you know where conversations are taking place about you, your product, or industry.

Why important: Using this information, you can make decisions as to where to deliver your message to your audience. You will also find out if the mentions are a result of your information being passed on by others, such as a "retweet" in Twitter. You can then determine the type of reach your message has.

➤ Area of mentions

It is helpful to know the area within your organization that people are discussing, such as:

- Customer service
- Product-related
- Sales
- Specific person within the company
- Accounting

What you learn: What areas of your company are being discussed more than others.

Why important: You can better determine who else in the company needs to provide support with your social media efforts. You also find out where to focus attention regarding your messaging and strategy and which tools you can use to appropriately address the issues.

Now that you are tracking mentions and are able to categorize them, you should plan how you are going to deal with them, particularly negative comments.

 TALES FROM THE ROAD

Bakery on Main
www.bakeryonmain.com

DO YOU MONITOR?

Yes, we monitor our own company and our competitors using Google Alerts. We have been able to find positive comments and reviews about our company and its products to help in promoting our brand on the web, and have been able to quickly respond to anything negative. That is really the most valuable part—to be able to connect with customers who aren't satisfied and publicly address their complaint so that others can see that we take all feedback, both good and bad, very seriously.

BIGGEST SUCCESS?

We are very new to social media, so we're still trying to find our way. But I think our biggest success was being able to get the word out that we were back in business after a fire in our bakery—not through a traditional press release, but through a silly YouTube video.

We distributed it to our trade and consumer email contacts and used our social media sites to spread it further and we got a great response from our customers. I think it was good to be able to show them that we are a small business and how happy we were to be making granola for them again.

PREPARING FOR WORST-CASE SCENARIO

Before you decide how to engage in social media, take some time to get organized and prepare for the worst. Every company hopes never to encounter a social media firestorm, but you need an "insurance policy" in place just in case. Even if you never run into problems, you will save precious time by having thought through the process and knowing how best to respond.

Let's look at the two things you need to consider:

- How to respond appropriately to comments, mainly the negative ones
- How to develop an internal policy covering usage of social media by employees

A walk through the chart

As you monitor your mentions and begin to engage people through your blog, social networks, and Twitter, you will deal with a variety of different people. For the most part, people will be positive and pleasant, but at some point you may need to respond to negative feedback.

➤ Trolls

Trolls are what I call people looking for trouble and trying to pick a fight. They are the ones who will leave a one-star review at Amazon.com when 500 other people left five-star reviews. Trolls create sites like walmartsucks.com. The good news is that most other people recognize Trolls for

Response Chart (based on Air Force Blog Assessment)

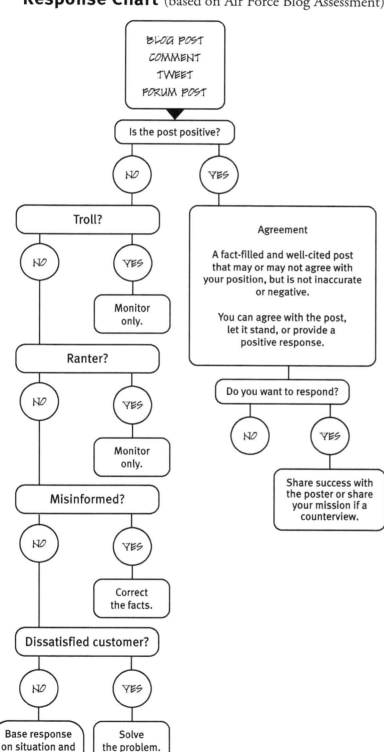

Response considerations:

➤ **Transparency**

Don't hide your association/company connection.

➤ **Sources**

Refer to sources to correct facts.

➤ **Timeliness**

Take your time to create an appropriate response, a few hours to a day.

➤ **Tone**

Stay neutral.

who they are and ignore them. Your job is to monitor trolls and keep a careful eye on them, but don't engage. They usually are extremists in nature, combative, and derogatory.

You may also find that these trolls use anonymous accounts to keep their true identity hidden. This secrecy allows them to say things that they normally wouldn't say because the ramifications are limited. You don't truly know their agenda or who they represent, which further puts you at a disadvantage—another reason to avoid engaging.

➤ Ranters

Ranters are usually found satirizing or making a joke about your product or company. Their behavior is not done to be malicious or overly negative. They just need to get something off their chest. Treat ranters like trolls—watch out for them, know what they're saying, but only engage them if absolutely necessary.

➤ Misinformed

Misinformed people have their facts wrong and are posting them as accurate. They probably mean no harm; they just have bad information. If this is the case, go ahead and engage them. Point them to sources with accurate information in a pleasant and neutral way. Don't be defensive. If you can direct them to a third-party source, that's even more effective than pointing them to your own site.

➤ Unsatisfied customers

Unsatisfied customers are frustrated about an experience they've had, and they're looking for assistance and a remedy to their situation. Maybe they have tried other ways to connect with your company and had no success, so now they are taking it online. You must engage these customers, apologize, and rectify the situation to the fullest extent you can. Your response will go a very long way toward transforming them into raving fans. Sometimes an unhappy customer can become a champion for you in your social media community.

Response considerations

➤ Be transparent

Social media is not for hiding your warts or using marketing spin. You need to be open about your messages, and invite your audience into your company and culture—warts and all. This is not to say you should give away the innermost secrets of your company—or the recipe for your restaurant's special sauce. I'm saying you should let the personal side of you and your company show through. It may seem strange and awkward at first, but you will find it becomes much more comfortable over time—and it's actually easier than constantly producing spin. Relax and have some fun.

➤ Cite sources

Many of the issues you encounter through negative comments will be rooted in inaccurate information often circulated online. As I mentioned earlier, it's easy to clear up these misunderstandings by citing sources that have the accurate information. The source could be on your site or blog or—even better—a third-party site, which will likely be viewed as more credible. In your comments, be sure to provide the link to the accurate information.

➤ Don't be late

You want to be timely in your response—but don't overreact. Once you discover a comment to investigate, check it out. Take the time to look at the entire conversation. Has anyone corrected the information for you already? If so, post a comment thanking everyone and offering any further assistance.

You shouldn't take more than a day to respond to a negative comment. If the comment is on an influencer's site, then the sooner you can respond the better. Just be sure to take the time to craft a professional response.

If you cannot respond in a timely manner—maybe there's a stock blackout period or you have to check with your legal department first—then let the community in on your process. Explain what is going on and when you plan to have a response. Silence is not always golden in these situations.

➤ Set the right tone

Don't take it personally—easier said than done, I know. The person leaving the comment is probably frustrated and/or emotional, and adding your emotions will only fan the flames. Remain as neutral in tone as possible when dealing with a negative comment. Take a deep breath and step away from the keyboard after reading the comment. Try to understand his or her side of the story and compose your response. If you're like me, you will have to edit it a couple of times to make it as neutral in tone as possible. Remember: your goal is to correct a situation and hopefully change the person from an angry commenter to a raving fan.

➤ Some other things to keep in mind

Know who in your company can respond to negative comments—and know how to reach them at any time. Negative comments can happen around the clock. If you allow them to fester over a weekend, you could have a really bad Monday morning when you return to the office.

As I mentioned in the discussion on timeliness, sometimes your community will come to your assistance. This situation is ideal. The negative commenter is more likely to believe someone not directly affiliated with your company. Be sure to thank those who came to your aid.

I said it before but it bears repeating: don't feed the trolls. They are just looking to pick a fight. Don't give them the satisfaction.

Just like the events that cause a spike in mentions, be aware that those same events can also cause an up-tick in negative comments:

- New product/service announcement or launch
- New advertising campaign or promotion
- Press release
- Event
- Product review
- News or blog article
- Product recall
- Competition

I hope you never have to reference this chapter again, but—if the unexpected happens—you will know what to do.

Internal policies

I'm going to start with a disclaimer. I am not a lawyer, so please have a lawyer review your employee policy to make sure it is legal.

Now that we've gotten that out of the way, let's talk about what a social media policy is, why you need one, and what to consider putting in the policy.

Not that long ago, companies were trying to figure out whether or not to allow employees to use the Internet and email at work. Now most companies have Internet usage as part of their employee handbooks. Social media is one more thing to consider.

➤ Why you need a policy

You need a policy to protect yourself and the company from an employee making negative comments or divulging secrets about your company, product, or customers online. I have heard of employees venting on their personal blogs about a problem client. If that client had ever seen these posts, the business would lose a major account. You need policies to keep your risk at a minimum.

A policy also allows for effective use of social media to benefit your company. You may have employees who are already active in social media, and their networks and communities could be an advantage to your company. By giving them guidelines for what they can and cannot say online, you create another evangelist who is empowered to spread your message.

In addition to policies, you also should provide training to employees so they are familiar with tools and privacy settings on popular sites. Provide them with disclaimers to be used on their personal blogs to show that their opinion does not reflect those of their employer.

➤ What to consider putting in your policy

- What disclaimers should your employees put on their personal profiles, if any? As I mentioned previously, it is a good idea to provide the exact wording you want your employees to use as disclaimers on their social media profiles and blogs.

- Define who at the company can use social media at work. Is everyone allowed to have access or only those who are engaging on behalf of the company? Consider writing responsibilities into your job descriptions.

- How should social media be used at work? Effective use of social media can be beneficial to a company, but using it for purely personal reasons and even playing games can be a major hit to productivity. Let people know what is allowed and what is not.

- Who is allowed to respond to comments? Consider creating a workflow for what happens when someone within the company comes across a comment that needs to be addressed. Not everyone should be able to respond unless they have been properly trained. Provide the contact information for those allowed to respond.

- What are the consequences for misuse of social media? This question is important. None of these policy items will matter if you do not enforce them when violated. If there is no enforcement and follow-through, people will not follow the policy at all.

- Address copyright issues and other legal issues. Whether it is your copyright or those of other companies, be careful to stay in compliance. If the employee is acting on your behalf, you ultimately will be held responsible. Train employees on the proper use of copyrights and how to provide credit when necessary.

- Address privacy issues. As with copyrights, you do not want to violate trust by publishing information that should remain private. If you want to talk about a client project in a blog, be sure to ask first for permission. Most clients will be happy, but you should always double-check. Provide guidelines to your staff so they know when and how to handle these issues.

➤ How to share your policy with employees

You have written your policy and have run it by a lawyer or your legal department. Now it is time to communicate the information throughout your organization. Here are some ideas to get you started:

- Handbook. If you have an employee handbook, you need to update it with your social media policy. If you don't have a handbook, you may want to create one. It doesn't have to be overly detailed, but such a resource is helpful when employees have questions about benefits, vacation, personal time, etc.

- Orientation training for new employees. When new employees begin, you may want to review your social media policy as part of their first day or orientation. Training on how to properly use the different tools could be a good idea as well.

- Workforce development for existing employees. If your staff is new to social media, you can provide some basic training on etiquette and the behaviors that are and aren't acceptable based on your policy.

- Person to serve as point of contact for issues and questions. As time goes on, questions are going to arise, so you want to identify someone within the organization as your social media resource. This person doesn't have to be in HR or IT; he or she can be the person responsible for social media for the company.

POTHOLES

CAUTION! Avoid:

- ➤ Going silent during a crisis while formulating your response.
- ➤ Feeding the trolls.
- ➤ Not having a response plan.
- ➤ Ignoring negative but constructive feedback.
- ➤ Not addressing incorrect information.
- ➤ Not creating a social media usage policy for employees.
- ➤ Not enforcing your employee policy.
- ➤ Not trusting your employees to be brand ambassadors.

TALES FROM THE ROAD

eRollover
www.erollover.com

DO YOU MONITOR?

Yes. We have been able to identify the needs of the different segments of our audience and develop our go-to market plan based on those insights.

WHAT WAS YOUR BIGGEST FEAR BEFORE STARTING WITH SOCIAL MEDIA – AND WAS THE FEAR WARRANTED?

Time management. We are still working to incorporate social media as the way each of us does our daily jobs.

Nomie Baby
www.nomiebaby.com

WHAT DO YOU KNOW NOW THAT YOU WISH YOU'D KNOWN BEFORE YOU DELVED INTO SOCIAL MEDIA?

I wish I had known more about keywords and linking and making the most out of connections.

WHAT WAS YOUR BIGGEST FEAR BEFORE STARTING WITH SOCIAL MEDIA – AND WAS THE FEAR WARRANTED?

I was worried that I was with everything out there and it would be difficult to be seen and heard. I was also afraid that I didn't get it and would make gaffes or social media faux pas.

TALES FROM THE ROAD CONTINUED...

Brewster House Bed and Breakfast

www.brewsterhouse.com

WHAT DO YOU KNOW NOW THAT YOU WISH YOU'D KNOWN BEFORE YOU DELVED INTO SOCIAL MEDIA?

It is important to learn to monitor, to scan, and to use alerts, rather than to attempt to read every posting—even by friends. However, there is no way that automated responses can create the relationships you can create via personal interaction.

WHAT WAS YOUR BIGGEST FEAR BEFORE STARTING WITH SOCIAL MEDIA - AND WAS THE FEAR WARRANTED?

Doing or saying something inappropriate that would cause others to stop following. It was warranted to a degree. It did not occur, but I think if you try to use social media as a direct marketing tool (so that every message is a sales pitch, however well-disguised) you will lose followers. If you try to be helpful and responsive to others, you need not worry that occasionally putting in a plug for the business will turn people off.

CHOOSING THE RIGHT TOOLS FOR THE JOB

We've talked about where you've been and where you want to go. You've listened and have a clear understanding of what you heard. You are even prepared for the worst. Now it is time to evaluate the tools that will help you reach your audience with the desired message.

Let's take a look at some of the different types of tools available to you:

- Blogs
- Social networks
- Microblogging
- Branded social networks
- Widgets/badges
- Multimedia
- Idea sharing
- Social media newsroom
- Location-based social networks

I will cover specific examples and suggestions for using each of these tools, as well as the pros and cons. Remember the goals we discussed in Chapter 5? I will discuss possible goals for each tool. You know social media can be time consuming, so I assign a "time rating" to each tool to help you decide which ones are a good fit. Finally, I will present some hints for moving forward with each tool.

As you review each tool, ask yourself if it can help you achieve the goals you have set. Be sure to complete the checklist at the end of each section.

Your blog

➤ Internal uses

To use a blog internally means that it is only accessible by people within your company, typically employees. If employees are one of your desired audiences, this tool should definitely be considered.

Project-based

Companies set up blogs to track a specific project, meaning there could be several blogs active at the same time. This type of blog tracks progress through a project, whether it be a move, inventory, or product development.

CEO

CEO blogs are authored by the owner or CEO and used to communicate to the staff. It's a great way to filter information to everyone and can also open up communications through employee comments. Having such a blog often reduces the amount of email sent throughout the company and keeps everyone on the same page.

Human Resources

These blogs are authored and managed by Human Resources and often cover information about policies, benefits, vacations, open positions, and other related information. Communicating changes to the company and allowing employees to respond with comments and questions goes a long way in supporting positive morale.

➤ External uses

External blogs target audiences beyond the walls of your company. These blogs are open to the public and may include:

CEO

The owner or CEO of the company is the blog's author. For a corporate example, check out Bill Marriott's blog (www.blogs.marriott.com). Marketing Roadhouse is also a CEO blog as far as definitions go, because I write it. You don't have to be a Fortune 500 company to have a CEO blog; you just have to be the author. These types of blogs typically fit well with the thought leadership goal.

Multiple blogs

Depending on your target markets and goals, you may find that you need more than one blog to get the job done. It may be a different blog per department or you may allow employees to have their own company-related blog like IBM does. It is critical to have some usage policies in place, but you can easily manage this task with the guidelines in Chapter 8.

Team approach

Some companies share the content responsibilities of the company blog. A great example is CRT/tanaka. One blog has six different authors, each with a different focus. Each author typically posts on a specific day to let readers know what to expect and when. One of my clients has spread the responsibilities over 11 different people to keep the time commitment to a minimum for each person. What makes this system work is that there is one point person who is responsible for keeping everyone on schedule and posting to the site.

Department

Depending on the goal of the blog and the audience, it is highly likely that an individual within a department will be responsible for most of the posting to the blog. The key is that one person is producing all the content with the exception of guest bloggers once and awhile. The voice of the company will come from this individual. The departments that typically manage this type of blog are marketing or communications.

➤ Pros

- A blog is more under your control and therefore more stable and reliable than free social networks and sites. This is why I always suggest that you pay for hosting and don't use a free blog service.

- The blog serves as the hub of your social media activity with other tools being used to promote your content and draw people to the blog. I will talk about hubs and spokes in more detail in the next chapter, but for now you need to understand that your hub will be used as the central tool to your social media strategy. Spokes will be used to promote and drive traffic to the hub.

- Blogs allow for larger amounts of content than most social networks. You are not limited to the amount of text you can post, meaning you can get your point across on your terms. You can also include images with the post to provide more context.

➤ Cons

- It can be difficult to create good and constant content. It is much better to focus on quality content on a consistent basis rather than decent content on a constant basis.

- There is often a cost to design, set up, and host your blog, depending on your skill set; however, it should cost less than your marketing website. Make sure the person you hire is familiar with building blogs because they are very different than a traditional website.

➤ Possible goals

- Thought leadership, which will position you as an expert in your field and helps to keep you "top of mind" when a prospect is ready to buy.

- Education or information for your audience on your industry, product, and company. This goal is similar to thought leadership and is often used in conjunction with it.

- Customer service. Helping people to use your product or service can go a long way toward keeping your customers loyal.

- Search Engine Optimization (SEO) is a process of optimizing your website to improve its ranking on search engines. Search engines love blogs because they are updated often and are full of keyword-rich content. While SEO is fine as a secondary goal, it should not be a primary goal. Creating great content that is useful to the reader is more important than stuffing keywords into your content.

- Event promotion. The biggest plus about using a blog for event promotion is that it provides content before, during, and after the event, which keeps people involved in the event at all stages.

➤ Amount of time needed: 8

(Scale of 1 to 10 with 10 being the most time-consuming)

- A greater amount of time is needed for creating content along with moderating and responding to comments than other tools. The upside is the time is a great investment.

➤ Hints

- Focus more on quality than quantity of your posts.

- Chunk your writing by creating multiple posts in one sitting and then space out your posting over the next week or month.

- Create an editorial calendar so you can plan your postings and not have to panic at the last minute about a topic. Look ahead at your month's activities and see what you can leverage for content.

- Read other sites and blogs to get ideas. You many want to share an article you found interesting and add your own commentary as your post.

POTHOLES

CAUTION! Avoid:

➤ Not allowing comments to be posted.

Should I consider using this tool?

Yes   /   No   /   Maybe

If yes or maybe, how will I use it?

_____

_____

_____

_____

Other people's blogs

Through monitoring and research you may have uncovered some blogs that cover your industry. These blogs provide you with a different set of opportunities.

➤ Uses

Comments

Commenting on blog posts written by other people is a great way to get to know other bloggers and their audience. The post does not have to be about your company for you to comment. It is great to become involved with a site and blogger to show your interest and thought leadership.

Blogger outreach

You may want to reach out to a blogger in hopes that he or she will write about you. Just like traditional media relations, you want to personalize your pitch to be effective. It always helps to know what the other bloggers write about and even comment a few times before sending a pitch.

Advertise/Sponsor

Many blogs sell advertising to make money, so if your target audience reads this blog, you may want to consider purchasing some ad space.

➤ Pros

- Through both leaving comments and advertising, you are able to drive people to your site if they want to learn more.

- Spending time on someone else's blog can be less time consuming than your own blog.

- It is easier to leverage an existing community than build your own. There is a fine line of getting involved with someone else's community and abusing the relationships, so tread lightly.

➤ Cons

- It can take time to find the correct blogs to comment on or buy advertising. You want to make sure it is the best fit for your audience and goals.

- Blogger relations require careful pitching or you risk being blogged about in a negative way. As I mentioned previously, learn what they write about and reach out in a personal way.

- The site is not in your control. While it is easier to get involved with an existing community, you will not have total control over your message.

- The blog's community will be less loyal to you than a community you establish with your own blog. Never underestimate the power of your own community.

➤ Possible goals

- Increase traffic to your website or blog through links in comments and/or advertising.

- Boost awareness to stay top of mind with your audience. You also look accessible to others because you are leaving comments.

- Your thought leadership position increases as you answer questions and provide your expert opinion.

- By responding to negative comments or questions, you can improve your overall customer service.

➤ Amount of time needed: 5

- If advertising, it is just a matter of finding the right site to sponsor or place ads.

- Blogger outreach takes more time to find blogs, learn about the blogger, and personalize the pitch.

- If you are only commenting on other blogs, your time investment will be based on monitoring for issues or direct reference to your company and/or product.

• Subscribe to blogs to learn when to comment with your expert opinion.

POTHOLES

CAUTION! Avoid:

➤ Improperly pitching to bloggers.

➤ Spamming comments on other blogs.

➤ Not commenting on other blogs.

Should I consider using this tool?

Yes / No / Maybe

If yes or maybe, how will I use it?

_____

_____

_____

_____

Social networks

There are more social networks than I can list. They range from the mainstream, like Facebook, to professional networks, such as LinkedIn, to niche networks like Eons for baby boomers.

These networks allow users to have profiles and share different types of information with friends and connections. Many also have opportunities for businesses to market themselves.

➤ Uses

Customers

Using social networks is a great way to connect with current customers and keep them up to date with what is happening at your company. It is often easier to connect with customers than prospects on social networks because customers already know and trust you and are much more likely to look for you online.

Advertise

Social networks have a deep understanding of their audience, which can be a huge advantage to you. If you find the social network where your target audience spends its time, buying advertising is a great investment.

Promote your blog

As I discussed earlier in the book, social media enables you to find your target audiences in the places where they spend most of their time. You can use these social networks to promote your blog by posting links for each post. If interested, users will click through and visit your blog.

➤ Pros

- The network already has built-in users to pull into your community. Facebook, for example, has more than 500 million people using their platform, so you have an opportunity to get in front of as many of those users as possible.

- Basic functions, such as profiles and pages, are pretty easy for most people to set up and maintain, which keeps your financial costs to a minimum.

- For the basic functionality, most social networks are free to use for both personal and business use.

- You do not have to create full blog posts as updates on social networks. Instead, share links to your blog, your website, or other third-party sites, as well as short updates and news.

- Social networks are not as fast-paced as microblogs, such as Twitter. The pace of Twitter can intimidate some people, so social networks may be closer to your comfort zone.

➤ Cons

- Social networks are not under your control, which can cause headaches if the site is down for maintenance or broken.

- You are subject to the social network's terms of service. You need to read, or at least skim, the terms to make sure that you keep ownership of your content, especially images.

➤ Possible goals

- Community building/networking

- Event promotion

- Increase traffic to site/blog

- Feedback from customers

- Thought leadership

➤ Amount of time needed: 5

➤ Hints

- Check back a few times a day since there are not usually notifications when users post an update or a comment.

- If you use the social network to invite others to your page, be sure to personalize invitations for business contacts so they can "connect the dots: as to how you know each other.

- Focus less on the numbers in the community and more on conversation and relevance.

POTHOLES →

CAUTION! Avoid:

➤ Setting up a profile and not a page.

➤ Sending all Twitter updates to Facebook.

➤ Sending all Facebook updates to Twitter.

Should I consider using this tool?

Yes   /   No   /   Maybe

If yes or maybe, how will I use it?

_____

_____

_____

_____

Microblogging

Microblogging refers to tools like Twitter. It limits the number of characters you can use in your post. In the case of Twitter, each post is limited to 140 characters. It may seem difficult at first, but you will quickly become comfortable with the limit.

➤ Uses

Sales

While you want to stay away from constant self-promotion, it is possible to create an account that is used specifically to sell. The caveat is you have to be upfront and open that this is the purpose of the account. I mentioned earlier in the book that Dell uses Twitter to sell inventory from its outlet store.

Customer support

Twitter is a great place to monitor for customer service issues. You are able to quickly and easily respond to people who have issues with your company and/or product.

Promote your blog

See a trend with this use? You will use every tool you can to promote your blog in order to increase your traffic.

➤ Pros

- The ability to set up keyword searches in Twitter makes it very easy to find people having conversations about topics of interest to you. From there, you can begin to follow and engage with those people.

- Twitter has a very simple account and profile set-up process.

- Creating and maintaining an account on Twitter is free, which makes it very accessible for many people to use.

➤ Cons

- It can be very easy to get sucked into Twitter and lose track of your time. You need to stay on track with your goals so you can get your other work accomplished.

- There is a bit of a learning curve with Twitter, from the 140-character limit to the semantics used to communicate with other users.

- The site is not within your control, meaning it could be unavailable when you need it. You'll see that I mention this con with other tools as well. Again, you need something reliable, such as your blog, to ensure your message is always available to your audience.

➤ Possible goals

- Increase traffic

- Thought leadership

- Networking

- Support

- Sales

- Customer feedback

➤ Amount of time needed:

- Set-up: 3

- Ongoing: 7 – 10. Depends on how you use the tool

➤ Hints

- If you have time-management issues, set a timer.

- Check your account at least three times a day to see if there is anything that requires a response. You also want to see what is being talked about so you can provide feedback.

- Set goals at first so you can determine the type of content to produce and post throughout each day.

POTHOLES →

CAUTION! Avoid:

➤ Keeping your profile/tweets set to private.

➤ Sending an automated direct message when someone follows you.

➤ Following someone only because you want that person to follow you.

➤ Ignoring mentions and direct messages.

Should I consider using this tool?

Yes   /   No   /   Maybe

If yes or maybe, how will I use it?

Branded social networks

Think of a branded social network as your own personal Facebook. It's a place where people who have an interest in your topic can engage with you and other like-minded individuals. Some examples of tools that allow you to create your social network are Ning, BuddyPress, and Webs.com.

Keep in mind that the network will not be specifically about your company but rather a subject in line with your expertise that others would find interesting and educational. Let's say you sell gluten-free cake mixes, so your social network may be about gluten-free cooking and food overall, not just your mixes.

➤ Uses

Resellers
If you have resellers for your product, they need to stay informed as to product development, promotions, and other tools. By creating a network where all of your resellers can learn from you as well as the other resellers, you have provided extra value to them.

Partners
Partners are similar to resellers in that they need to be privy to internal information. These partners may provide complementary services to your product or service to be able to bring more value to your clients.

Customers
Depending on your offerings, your customers may find a branded social network useful—especially if you provide information beyond your offering, as in my previous example about the gluten-free cake mix company. Educate and provide value beyond your product.

Employees

I truly see branded social networks to be the new intranet for companies. These networks will be located behind the firewall, like an intranet, but will make it easier for employees to interact with each other.

➤ Pros

- Your own social network gives you a dedicated network for conversations with your audience. It also allows your audience to interact and learn from each other.

- You get a little more control of your branding and messaging with your own social network. You can brand it with your logo and other elements.

➤ Cons

- Unlike setting up profiles on other social networks, it is more difficult to set up your own network. While there are tools that make it easy, it still requires more effort.

- Keeping the network fresh and updated with content can be really difficult, but it's absolutely necessary to keep your community truly engaged so they return often to see what is new.

- Building your community can be difficult depending on the target audience. Customers will need to be convinced by your content to sign up for "one more social network." If you provide content they cannot find elsewhere, your efforts will be successful.

➤ Possible goals

- Feedback for users

- Build community

- Networking

➤ Amount of time needed:

- Set-up: 7. Some services may make set-up easier, but there is still a bit of time involved.

- Ongoing: 9. Requires more frequent content than blogs to keep people coming back and interacting.

➤ Hints

- If you can get your community involved with each other, then you can step back.

Should I consider using this tool?
Yes / No / Maybe

If yes or maybe, how will I use it?

_____

_____

_____

_____

Widgets

A widget is a stand-alone application that people easily pull from your site and place on their own blogs or social media profiles. Services that host and help you create these widgets are KickApps, Gigya, and Widgetbox.

➤ Uses

Promote events

If you are planning an event, you can provide a widget to exhibitors and attendees so they are able to announce their involvement.

Entertain

Widgets become very popular when the content of the widget is entertaining and interactive.

➤ Pros

- Can be truly viral, which means your message will be passed on from site to site, giving you more exposure.

- Allows others to promote you and/or your content on their own site, blog, or social network profile. Having a third-party promote you is always more credible than self-promotion.

- There is measurement with some widget platforms, so you can track how many people have installed the application on their site.

➤ Cons

- You will most likely need outside help to develop a widget.

- Once created, it is out of your control with regard to who puts your widget where, which could lead to guilt by association.

➤ Possible goals

- Boost awareness

- Education

- Event promotion

➤ Amount of time needed:

- Set-up: 6. Depends on the sophistication of the widget and who develops it.

- Ongoing: 2. Content is automatically pushed via RSS, so most work is from tracking placements, which is easy.

➤ Hints

- The more interesting the content, the more likely others will share and place it on their blogs or social network profiles.

Should I consider using this tool?

Yes   /   No   /   Maybe

If yes or maybe, how will I use it?

_____

_____

_____

_____

Multimedia

Multimedia, which includes audio, video, and pictures, can be used in many different ways throughout social media. Some media has its very own social network (video on YouTube and photos on Flickr), but they can also be used in conjunction with your other tools.

➤ Uses

There really are a million ways to utilize multimedia in your social media strategy. It can stand alone on sites dedicated to that type of media, or it can be embedded into your website, blog, or social networks.

Hosted media

What I am talking about here is creating different types of media that can then be hosted on other sites, such as:

- Video on YouTube or Vimeo
- Pictures and video on Flickr
- Powerpoint presentations on SlideShare

Podcast

A podcast can be an audio or video file. What truly makes it different is the fact that people subscribe to it just like they would your blog. Your podcast can be hosted at iTunes and downloaded to be listened to on an MP3 player or computer. Podcasts typically are produced on a regular basis like a television or radio show.

Live media

In addition to stored audio or video, you can also stream live information to people through tools like Ustream for video and BlogTalk Radio for audio. These are great tools for an announcement or for doing a show regularly to increase your thought leadership.

➤ Pros

- Media does not have to be professionally produced. Amateur video is preferred and seen as more real and trusted.

- An easy-to-use inexpensive camera reduces your time and cost.

- Your company seems more human and approachable.

➤ Cons

- Can be difficult if you are camera shy.

- Slight learning curve if you are not used to working with video or audio files.

➤ Possible goals

- Education

- Boost awareness

- Event promotion

- Thought leadership

➤ Amount of time needed:

- Set-up: 5 to 10. Depends on how much preparation, shooting, and post-production work is needed.

- Ongoing: 3. After posting, you just need to monitor for comments.

➤ Hints

- Do some planning to make sure video or audio flows well.

- Think about doing transcripts to include captioning in videos for individuals who are hearing impaired.

Should I consider using this tool?

Yes / No / Maybe

If yes or maybe, how will I use it?

_____

_____

_____

_____

Idea sharing

Think of it as an online suggestion box where people can suggest features or provide feedback. Idea sharing can be used by customers to provide feedback on a current product, future product, or company operations. Salesforce.com, SuggestionBox.com, and GetSatisfaction.com provide tools for idea sharing.

➤ **Uses**

Focus group

Instead of inviting a group of people to talk in person about your product, you can set up a real-time, online focus group. When people like your brand, they want to feel involved in your product. Giving them the opportunity to be involved provides a sense of ownership.

Improve product

Sure you will encounter a few trolls, but for the most part people want to help you improve your company and product. Their point of view may be fresher than an internal one, which will offer you many opportunities for growth.

➤ Pros

- The cost of getting this kind of feedback is much less than a traditional focus group.

- You gain strong insight on what people want from your company and your product/service.

➤ Cons

- Negative feedback can be difficult to accept.

- You must be willing to act upon relevant feedback.

➤ Possible goals

- Improve customer service.

- Encourage customer input/feedback.

➤ Amount of time needed:

- Set-up: 5. Online services make it easy to set up.

- Ongoing: 8. You should check at least once a day to read posts and respond.

- Don't use this tool unless you are willing to listen and act upon feedback.

Should I consider using this tool?
Yes   /   No   /   Maybe

If yes or maybe, how will I use it?

_____

_____

_____

_____

Social media newsroom

Often built on the same software as a blog, this content is more focused on posts about the company rather than education/thought leadership. A social media newsroom can replace a news section on the company website and can coexist with a blog. In addition to news releases, these newsrooms often include bios, headshots of the owners, and logos. As with a blog, a mix of media is effective.

➤ Uses

Media relations

Reporters frequently research companies and are on the lookout for sources. By having the information they need when they need it, you can become a go-to source for the reporter.

Blogger relations

Similar to reporters, bloggers often research companies for a post. If the information they need is readily available, they are more likely to include you.

➤ Pros

- Does not require as many frequent posts as a blog.

- Frees up requests for bios, logos, and headshots.

- Allows press to follow you by subscribing to your RSS feed.

➤ Cons

- Doesn't provide the expert/thought leadership of a blog.

- Harder to set up than a blog because there are not a lot of templates available.

➤ Possible goals

- Media relations

➤ **Amount of time needed:**

- Set-up: 7. Building the site may require outside help.

- Ongoing: 6. Posts are created as news is released and needs to be distributed.

➤ **Hints**

- Mix in multimedia.

- Link to other social media accounts.

Should I consider using this tool?

Yes / No / Maybe

If yes or maybe, how will I use it?

_____

_____

_____

_____

Location-based social media

A new trend is GPS-based social networks, which require an individual to be in a specific physical location to participate. Examples include Foursquare, Gowalla, BrightKite, Whrrl, and Facebook Places.

➤ Uses

The true opportunities in this area are yet to be seen as it is a relatively new market used mainly by early adopters.

Reward loyal customers

The most logical use is to reward those who frequent your business the most and check in on the network.

➤ Pros

- Creating a special offer for one of the networks is easy and does not require any involvement on the site. You can simply post a sign in your establishment.

- It is free to sign up and participate, both as a business and a user.

➤ Cons

- Low participation right now, mainly early adopters.

- Ever-changing landscape. There is no clear-cut leader as of yet.

➤ Possible goals

- Foster customer loyalty.

➤ Amount of time needed:

- Set-up: 3. Choose site to use, the reward to give, and post it.

- Ongoing: 2. Reward those who achieve your goal.

➤ Hints

- Look and listen to find out which site is popular in your area.

- Sign up and play first so you can get used to how it works.

- Have fun with it to create interest.

Should I consider using this tool?

Yes / No / Maybe

If yes or maybe, how will I use it?

_____

_____

_____

_____

Now that you have been introduced to some social media tools, it is time to make some decisions and get to work.

TALES FROM THE ROAD

Elena Adams Designs
www.elena-adams.com

WHAT DO YOU KNOW NOW THAT YOU WISH YOU'D KNOWN BEFORE YOU DELVED INTO SOCIAL MEDIA?

When I first started using social media, I thought it was important to propel the image that I was a professional business. With use I've realized that people are far less interested in just seeing links and marketing talk, and really just want to connect with others. By blending promotion with a much more personal, micro-blogging style, and including links to things I simply find interesting that are related to my industry, I've built a more solid group of followers.

WHAT ADVICE WOULD YOU SHARE WITH OTHER BUSINESSES THAT ARE JUST GETTING STARTED WITH SOCIAL MEDIA?

Just being there isn't enough. So many businesses start a page, make a few basic posts and then rarely return. They seem to treat a lot of these sites like old-school, static websites, leaving posts like "check out our website" or "come back soon for more." I don't remember the last time I actually opened someone's profile. If they aren't appearing in my stream, then they might as well not exist.

Decide how much time you want to give over to each site and stick with it. Just like with any advertising, a steady drip of involvement is infinitely better than a one-time effort. I aim for one to two tweets per day and one Facebook post every three days.

PUTTING IT ALL TOGETHER

In the last nine chapters, you've learned about the pieces to the social media puzzle. Now it's time to put all those pieces together and see the big picture.

Like I mentioned in Chapter 1, everyone who reads this book has different pieces and thus a different picture. There will be some similarities, of course, but—just like a fingerprint or snowflake—no two will be exactly alike. There is no true cookie-cutter method or one-size-fits-all approach to social media—and beware of those who offer you such a product. It won't produce the results you seek. I can lead you down a path of thinking, but ultimately you are responsible for choosing your final destination. You will likely encounter some trial and error along your path, but you will find your way.

As you begin to put your pieces together, try thinking about your social media strategy in terms of a hub and spoke model—with the hub being a site that is easy to update, updated frequently, and under your control. Your hub will typically be either a blog or a social media newsroom. Both are built on a Content Management System (CMS), which allows you to easily update the site without the assistance of IT or your website developer. This ease of updating also means you will be able to update your hub more frequently than your website. How often you update will depend on which type of hub you select and your editorial calendar, which we will discuss in Chapter 12.

Your hub should be within your control. And that means you are going to have to pony up some money, get a hosting plan that includes blogging software (try WordPress), and set up your blog or newsroom there. Yes, there are free services, but have you ever truly read their terms of service? Who owns your content once it is uploaded? What happens if they go out of business? What about downtime? You will probably experience some downtime with your hosting company—but, since you are paying for the service, the company will want to limit that downtime. And because you pay, the likelihood of the company shutting down services with no warning is minimal. The same cannot be said for free services. It's not my intention to scare you but to provide you with the facts so you can make informed decisions.

Another important reason to consider hosting your own blog is that you will have more control over its appearance and features. The free services limit what you can do to customize your site, which may hamper your branding and communications. I have also known blogs to be shut down without warning because they are labeled as spam due to some of the language they use on their blog, such as "free" and "coupons." I'm a bit of a control freak when it comes to my online presence, so I like to pay a little extra to get exactly what I want in terms of appearance and functionality.

So now it's decision time. What will you use as a hub? Still not sure? Ask yourself a few questions:

	A	B
I WANT TO CREATE CONTENT THAT IS...	EDUCATIONAL AND NOT JUST ABOUT MY BUSINESS	ALL RELATED TO MY BUSINESS
MY UPDATES WILL BE...	WEEKLY	EVERY FEW WEEKS
MY GOAL IS...	BUILD COMMUNITY AND THOUGHT LEADERSHIP	PROVIDE COMPANY INFORMATION

If you answered more As, then a blog is the way for you to go. If you answered mostly Bs, then a newsroom is the better choice. Most people will go with a blog because it gives you more flexibility and is more in line with your goals. A newsroom is better suited for companies that produce a lot of news and aren't as interested in engaging with their audience. Some companies actually have both a blog and newsroom because they serve very different goals and audiences.

Write down what kind of site you will use as your hub:

_____

Now that you have your hub, we can talk about the spokes. The spokes surround the hub and are used to deliver the hub's message to your target audiences where they like to spend their time. How do we know where that is? Through your monitoring and research, right? Deliver the desired message to your target audiences where they are. If you make your message compelling enough, they will visit your hub and subscribe to get future updates.

Remember: all of your spokes do not need to deliver the same message. You can change the message for each audience. One spoke may target Audience A, while another spoke targets Audience B.

Another thing to consider with regard to your spoke options is whether the spoke will be used as a campaign or on an ongoing basis. Maybe you have an ad campaign or event that you want to promote separately from your daily message. Think about the Body by Milk ads. This campaign is from America's Milk Processors, just as the Milk Mustache campaign is. A campaign usually has an end date and a very specific theme-oriented message. Ongoing messages are usually more company-based and general in nature.

Depending on the type of business you have, you may need different pages or accounts for different products or uses. Maybe you have one product that is for horses and another that is for dogs. The products have the same basic ingredients, but they differ in how they're used and by whom. Appealing to two different audiences may be difficult on the same account or page, so it might be best to create two different pages.

Does this approach require more work? Maybe at first, but you may also find it is easier to produce very specific content for each group rather than general information that works for both. The reward is potentially a highly engaged community that helps you produce content and conversation over time.

Take another look at the last chapter and write down all the tools that you marked with Yes or Maybe:

1. _____

_____

2. _____

_____

3. _____

_____

4. _____

_____

5. _____

_____

I would suggest that you not implement all of these—and especially not all at once. We'll talk about rolling out your strategy in a moment, but let's finalize it first. Answer the following questions for each tool you just put in your Yes/Maybe spoke list:

Tool 1

Tool type: _____

_____

Tool name: _____

_____

How will you use it? _____

_____

Which audience(s) will you target? _____

_____

What message will you deliver? _____

_____

What is your goal? What do you want to accomplish? _____

_____

Will this be ongoing or a campaign? _____

_____

Will it be company- or product-based? _____

Tool 2

Tool type: _____

_____

Tool name: _____

_____

How will you use it? _____

_____

Which audience(s) will you target? _____

_____

What message will you deliver? _____

_____

What is your goal? What do you want to accomplish? _____

_____

Will this be ongoing or a campaign? _____

_____

Will it be company- or product-based? _____

Tool 3

Tool type: _____

_____

Tool name: _____

_____

How will you use it? _____

_____

Which audience(s) will you target? _____

_____

What message will you deliver? _____

_____

What is your goal? What do you want to accomplish? _____

_____

Will this be ongoing or a campaign? _____

_____

Will it be company- or product-based? _____

Tool 4

Tool type: _____

_____

Tool name: _____

_____

How will you use it? _____

_____

Which audience(s) will you target? _____

_____

What message will you deliver? _____

_____

What is your goal? What do you want to accomplish? _____

_____

Will this be ongoing or a campaign? _____

_____

Will it be company- or product-based? _____

Tool 5

Tool type: _____

_____

Tool name: _____

_____

How will you use it? _____

_____

Which audience(s) will you target? _____

_____

What message will you deliver? _____

_____

What is your goal? What do you want to accomplish? _____

_____

Will this be ongoing or a campaign? _____

_____

Will it be company- or product-based? _____

Still not 100 percent sure what to use? Then go mainstream with a blog, Facebook, and Twitter.

Rollout plan

You've identified the tools you'll use to deliver your message to your target audiences. Now you need to plan how you are going to implement these tools. As I stated earlier, you don't want to roll out every tool at the same time because it would be overwhelming.

By launching one tool at a time, you can get a feel for that tool, find your voice, get comfortable with the routine, and have some fun with it. This process should not add more stress to your job; you need to be open to the trial and error and be patient enough to give your community time to develop. The last thing you want is a "tumbleweed account"—a tool that has been used for two weeks and then left for dead, blowing through the streets of social media.

Take one tool at a time, get your feet wet, then dive in and start swimming.

Because your hub will be the center of all your activity it is best to get that set up first. Depending on how much customization you want and your skill set, this task could also take the largest amount of time to complete.

Let's assume you have selected your blog as your hub. There are many free and inexpensive themes available to

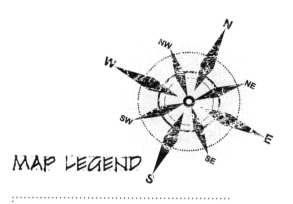

MAP LEGEND

EXAMPLE OF PREMIUM
WORDPRESS THEMES:

WooThemes
http://www.woothemes.com/

Headway
http://headwaythemes.com/

Thesis
http://diythemes.com/

give you a good-looking blog very quickly. You may need to hire someone to set up and develop your blog.

As you build your hub, make sure you designate space for links to all your spoke sites. These links serve two purposes, allowing people to:

- Find other ways to connect with you. Individuals can then choose the tools they use most often to stay connected.

- Verify that you are who you say you are. For example, someone finds your Twitter account but wants to make sure it is your official account and not a fake. They will click on the bio link of your profile. This link should take them to your hub. On the hub, they should be able to easily find the link back to the Twitter account. From that, they are able to confirm that your Twitter account is legitimate.

Once your hub is all set up and ready to go, start adding a few posts as you are setting up your spokes. People want to see the type of content your blog will have the first time they visit, so provide a good taste of the kind of information you will be sharing. Give them about three posts to check out before you heavily promote your blog.

Which spokes, how many you use, and when you start using them will be determined by your:

- Experience with each tool

- Target market—audiences who know you versus those who don't

- Resources, mostly time and money

➤ Experience

You may already have some personal experience with one or more of the tools you have selected to use. While business versus personal content will definitely be different, most of the functionality will be the same. This familiarity will help you worry less about the technology so you can focus more on the content and conversation.

If you do not have experience with any of the tools, then start with a tool that you can ease into slowly—like a social network. Consider using it on a personal level first before jumping in for business for the very reason mentioned previously—comfort. It's better to make a few mistakes on your personal account before moving onto your business account.

➤ Target audiences

You've selected the audiences to target, and you know which tools you are going to use to reach them. It's a good idea to start with the tools that will target the audiences who already know you and like you, such as customers and partners.

It is easier to engage these people because there is already a level of trust, which makes it more likely they will engage with you. The best part of starting with your loyal audience is that they will become the foundation for your community. They will often jump in to answer questions and provide assistance when you aren't able, which is a huge advantage to you.

➤ Resources

Let's consider the two resources that are most important to any business—time and money. Look at each of the tools you've selected and evaluate how much time and money are involved with set-up and ongoing usage.

I feel that experience and target market will influence your decision more than available time, but time is still a factor to consider. Look at your current schedule and determine what time you can devote to executing your plan effectively.

Money is a different issue. You shouldn't go broke implementing your social media strategy. Create a budget line item for social media and make the most of it.

POTHOLES

CAUTION! Avoid:

➤ Not having a hub as part of your social media strategy.

➤ Jumping in with too many tools at once and burning out.

TALES FROM THE ROAD

YouCanDoWhatYouLove.com
www.ycdwyl.com

BIGGEST CHALLENGE?

Balancing time. It is easy to get caught up in the ins and outs of social media and let other things go by the wayside; alternately, it can be the perfect procrastination tool. Really you can spend as much or little time with these avenues as you like, but the key is to figure out what is working and focus on one or two sites, making your time on them valuable and productive. It can seem like a waste of time for your own company if you promote other users who you support, but these are the types of connections that move you forward, so a healthy dose of "give and take" is worth your time.

WHAT ADVICE WOULD YOU SHARE WITH OTHER BUSINESSES THAT ARE JUST GETTING STARTED WITH SOCIAL MEDIA?

Social media is a form of networking as much as a dinner for your local business alliance or alumni association, with the ability to span internationally. The essential word to keep in mind is "balance:" 1) Keep a "balance" of networking online as much as networking face-to-face. 2) When interacting with others, keep a "balance" of give and take. If you support another business that can benefit your readers, the readers will find you even more helpful—and the business you supported is more likely to return the favor by promoting you as well, giving you the ability to reach a new audience.

IMPLEMENTING THE TOOLS

Now it's time to get the tools you've selected ready for action.

I'm not going to go into detail on how to implement every tool that is available for you to use in social media. If I did, you would need to carry this book around in a wheelbarrow. Instead, I want to focus on what you need to know to properly implement your blog. Even if you get outside help to build your blog, you will need this information to work with your web developer.

Free versus self-hosted blog

You have many options for the platform to use when building your blog. You can go the free route of TypePad, Blogger, and WordPress.com. TypePad also has a pro option for a monthly fee. Many hosting companies support my favorite blogging platform, which is the WordPress self-hosted option. For the price of monthly hosting, you get your own WordPress blog after a simple install. Let me explain why I think it is worth investing a few dollars a month to have a self-hosted blog.

➤ Control

You get more overall control over your blog if you go the self-hosted route than a free service. Think about it—if service providers are giving you something for free, then they want to limit what you can do. I have heard complaints from people using Blogger about how often features and functionality change, making it difficult to use the service. You need to read carefully the terms of service for these sites to make sure that you retain the rights to your content or that you won't be blocked for mistakenly being viewed as spam. These issues can also arise with Facebook. Just be careful what you agree to when using free services.

➤ Reliability

Nothing, I repeat nothing, on the Internet is 100 percent reliable, but when you pay someone for hosting they work very diligently to keep your site up and running as much as possible—and most of them do a pretty good job at it. A free service wants to stay up as much as possible too, but let's face it. The motivation is a little different. If your blog goes down, you want to be able to call someone and know when it will be back up and running. There is no one to call at Blogger; you just sit and wait—not a good feeling when you are trying to run a business.

Another aspect of reliability is longevity. How long will companies continue to offer a free service? This situation already happened with Ning when the company dropped its free option. People had built communities using Ning and now need to pay to keep them active. It's not long until other services follow this lead and cut their free service in efforts to increase revenue for their stakeholders. Even worse is if a service decides to totally shut down, leaving you to scramble for an alternate solution and possibly losing the connection with readers you have worked so hard to nurture.

➤ Customization

An important part of integrating social media with the rest of your marketing efforts is to keep consistent branding throughout all your marketing tools. For this reason, being able to customize your blog's design with your branding is very important. While the free services give you some design customization options, it's not nearly as flexible as a self-hosted blog. The free services also limit your use of plug-ins and widgets that allow you to improve the experience of your readers. From a technical point of view, I completely understand why they do this, but it can be frustrating from an aesthetic and marketing point of view.

I know I have bashed the free services, but that's just my point of view. It's not to say that free services are bad. They definitely have their place. I just feel strongly that if you are a business intent on putting your best foot forward, then you should evaluate if saving that money is worth it in the long run.

Blog appearance

There are numerous options when it comes to picking a theme to use with your blog. The main decision to make is whether to use a free theme or pay for one. All you have to do is a simple Google search on "free WordPress themes" or "premium WordPress themes" to see all of your options. In building blogs for clients, I have had experience with both free and premium themes, and my best experiences have been with premium. Keep in mind that the premium themes almost always cost less than $100, which is a small price to pay to make life easier.

Here are the advantages of a premium theme:

- You can get support from the developer if you do have a problem.

- You may have a footer with the developer name, but you won't have other unrelated links in the footer that you can't remove. Free themes often put links in the footer to sites selling something. Because they are free, you are not allowed to remove these.

- Easy-to-use control panels make for simpler and faster customization and changes.

- Free theme updates to match changes to WordPress.

Once you have selected your theme and installed and customized it, you should add a few more things to your blog. First you want to add an About or Author page—not a post, a page. You want people to know who is behind the writing of the blog. It helps to give the reader a better feel for the voice of the author or authors. Be sure to include all your authors if it is a team blog. In addition to short bios, try to include a photo.

The final thing you need to have on your blog are links to both your company's website and any social media spokes you are using. Providing this info results in two benefits to you and your readers. One, it lets people know other ways to connect with you, such as Twitter or Facebook. Different people prefer different social media tools, so if you link to them on your blog they are able to choose how they want to stay connected. The second advantage is that if people find you on Twitter and want to make sure you are, in fact, legitimate, it helps to have links that cross-pollinate so they will know you are who you say you are.

Note: I refer to WordPress self-hosted edition because I have the most experience with this platform and prefer it. You can apply most of this information to the platform of your choosing.

Subscriptions

One great thing about blogs is the ability to allow people to subscribe to your updates. The vehicle for this feature is Real Simple Syndication (RSS). Blogs come with this functionality standard, but I like to use a free third-party solution, such as Feedburner, to manage my subscriptions for me.

In addition to RSS, Feedburner allows your readers to subscribe to your feed via email, which is important because some people are much more comfortable with email. About one half of my subscribers use the email option to stay up to date with my blog. If I didn't have email subscription as an option, I might not reach this audience. Depending on your target market, you may find this percentage to be even higher.

Feedburner's email subscription option also gives you the ability to customize the subject line and fonts and add a logo to the email. Beyond the appearance, my favorite customization is defining when the email should be delivered to the reader's inbox. As you go, you will probably play with the best time of day to publish a post until you get a feel for what works well. Once you know this information, you can set your email to go out in that two-hour timeframe.

The last thing I want to mention about Feedburner is related to the analytics it provides. This information shows you how many subscribers you have on a daily basis and breaks down how people are accessing your feed by showing which reader or if it is via email subscription. The analytics also show you which posts are the most accessed on a given day.

Managing comments

One of the first things I hear from clients when we begin to discuss a blog is, "I don't want to allow comments." I understand the concern about someone saying something bad about you or the company; it's legitimate. It's new for a lot of companies to be that open to direct criticism in a public forum. They are used to dealing with these issues behind the scenes, whether it is on the phone, in person, or even through email. What they don't realize is they still may be criticized through other social media avenues, so I feel it's better to have it take place on your blog where you can fully respond.

I'm a firm believer in allowing comments on a blog. There are a few exceptions to this rule, but for the most part companies need to be willing to open themselves to conversation. By not allowing comments, the company sends a message of being closed off to their audience and most likely will not enjoy much success.

I offer two bits of advice to clients to help ease their apprehension—one is to create a comments policy and the second is to choose an option for comments moderation. The use of a comments policy gives you a little control over being able to remove the trolls from your blog. If you have a policy that people can read and you can enforce, you can deal with trolls who are just out to cause trouble and offer no true value to the conversation.

With regard to comments moderation, you can choose how comments get posted to your blog. WordPress gives you three options:

- Let every comment automatically post to the blog.

- Every comment must be approved before posting to the blog.

- Approve the comment author the first time and then future comments from that author will be automatically posted.

I prefer and recommend the third option. If someone leaves a legitimate comment the first time, then his or her future comments probably will be legitimate too. Approving once at the beginning allows for more real-time conversation and a little less effort on your part. As an add-on to this idea, you should also try to be close to your blog's dashboard when you publish a new post so that you can approve comments quickly. It can be very frustrating to people who post a comment to wait for it to be posted. It stifles the conversation and turns people off from leaving comments in the future.

Comment tool box

Now let's talk a little about the technical options for comments. I want to mention three plug-ins that, in my opinion, enhance comments and therefore your blog.

The first plug-in you cannot live without is Akismet for managing comment spam. Yes, like everything else, the spammers have discovered blogs are another way to let you know about their wonderful enhancement products. If you don't have this plug-in installed, you will have to wade through all the spam to find the legitimate comments. I will caution that sometimes a legitimate comment gets caught in the filter so you should check it from time to time. Believe me, this plug-in is a huge timesaver.

Like most bloggers, I love to get comments on my blog, but sometimes find it difficult to respond to people because of the standard format of comments. I love the idea of threaded conversations in comments and Disqus can give you this functionality. From a user standpoint, it allows you to set up a Disqus profile, which keeps track of where you leave comments and any responses to your comments. This plug-in is especially helpful to keep track of what you have said and if you need to return for additional comments. From a blogger standpoint, it allows your commenters this same functionality and makes responding to each individual much easier.

The last plug-in I want to mention is CommentLuv, which is really about giving a little bonus to your readers who leave a comment. This plug-in links to the latest blog post of the comment author, allowing the reader to promote his or her own work and perhaps even increasing the likelihood of the reader leaving a comment in the first place.

Blog and social media newsroom checklist *(hub)*

☐ RSS feed subscription

☐ Email subscription option

☐ Google Analytics or your preferred analytics tool *(This will be covered in Chapter 14)*

☐ About section to introduce writer(s)

☐ Header graphic with logo and image

☐ Headshot of writer

☐ Links to main website

☐ Links to social media accounts *(spokes)*

☐ Description of what readers may find on the blog/newsroom

☐ Contact information

Social network profile checklists *(spokes)*

Like I said before, with so many different social media tools and sites available, I cannot cover them all in this book. I have created a short list of items that are typically needed to set up accounts or profiles on most of these sites. If you have these items ready to go, it should streamline your efforts.

- ☐ Profile picture (could be a logo, your building, headshot, or an icon that illustrates your business, such as a sock monkey for a toy store). It should be something that people will recognize and associate with your business.

- ☐ Description of your business. Try to make this keyword specific for your business since people frequently search on topics that interest them.

- ☐ Photos, if permitted by the social network. People love to look and comment on pictures, so consider adding some.

- ☐ Blog and website URLs. You are using these spokes to drive people to your hub so be sure to include these URLs to get them there.

Integration

There are many opportunities to integrate your social media accounts, enabling you to post the same message to multiple accounts at the same time. While this convenience may seem tempting, consider the following:

- Different sites may have different semantics. An RT or @ on Twitter won't make sense on Facebook.

- You may have the same people on multiple networks, so you may want to stagger posts so you don't overwhelm.

- Some integration can actually annoy your audience. Going from Facebook to Twitter is easy but annoys Twitter users because it sends an unnecessary link along with the tweet.

- Some social media tools are more conversational than others, so be aware of pushing conversations that may not have context on the sites where the conversation is not taking place.

Integrate accounts when it makes sense and not to make it easier on yourself. Some examples of when integration makes sense include:

- You are sharing a link to your blog post or an article on someone else's site.

- It is an announcement or statement under 140 characters, if Twitter is being used.

- The post doesn't contain semantics specific to one of the networks.

Scheduling posts/updates

Everyone is busy so if you can save a little time and still share great content, why wouldn't you? Many tools allow you to schedule your posts to be sent at a later time.

Maybe you have found a lot of links to share but you want to spread them out throughout the day or even week. By setting them up to auto-post at a given time, you are still sharing content when away from the computer or busy with projects or clients.

Another favorite of mine is being able to connect my blog's RSS feed to Facebook Notes so it will automatically post to Facebook without any further involvement from me.

Helper tools

Third-party application developers have created several helper tools that make accomplishing your social media activities much easier. (Trust me, if you had to use Twitter solely via its website on a daily basis, you wouldn't use it for long.)

These tools usually come down to personal preference, so the one you ultimately choose may be different from

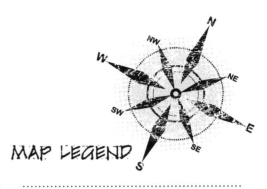

MAP LEGEND

HELPER TOOLS

- HootSuite
  www.hootsuite.com

- TweetDeck
  www.tweetdeck.com

- Seesmic
  www.seesmic.com

- Ping.fm
  www.ping.fm

everyone else. You need to evaluate the features that are most important to you and then find the tools that best meet your needs.

CAUTION! Avoid:

➤ Making irregular updates on your hub and spokes.

➤ Using the default profile picture the site gives you.

➤ Not making it easy to subscribe to your blog.

➤ Turning comments off on your blog.

 TALES FROM THE ROAD

The Grammar Doctors
www.grammardocs.com

WHAT ADVICE WOULD YOU SHARE WITH OTHER BUSINESSES THAT ARE JUST GETTING STARTED WITH SOCIAL MEDIA?

Plan it into your day. Too many people think it's a waste of time, but if you're making money and being seen as an expert, it's not. You only need about an hour a day to really be effective.

Help My Resume
www.helpmyresume.org

WHAT ADVICE WOULD YOU SHARE WITH OTHER BUSINESSES THAT ARE JUST GETTING STARTED WITH SOCIAL MEDIA?

Companies first need to understand that social media is not a technique used to make a hard sell on initial contact. If implemented correctly, with an attitude of engagement and listening, the following will occur and your business and ROI will grow:

- Increased brand awareness

- Reputation management

- Improved search engine rankings

- Increased relevant visitor traffic

- Improved sales for a product or service

PUTTING THE PLAN INTO ACTION

You have the plan and you have the tools, so finally it is time to jump in and engage. For some of you, this part will come very naturally while others may struggle. With a little practice, you will find your voice, as well as what content works best with your audience.

Use this chapter as a guide to get started. Remember, there is no cookie-cutter solution. Content follows the same rule. I can provide ideas and guidelines, but you will need to discover the specific content that works best for you. It can take a little bit of trial and error to find the perfect fit. You will also find that things are constantly evolving, so what may have worked last month is less effective this month. Do not get discouraged. You will find your voice, and your community will follow and engage.

If you are struggling with ideas, start with some of the following:

➤ Use your inbox as inspiration

Keep an eye on the questions that drop into your inbox, and see if you can compose a blog post to respond to the question. Doing so provides you with two benefits: you have a great blog post and, in the future, you can point to this post when asked the question again. Let's face it, you will be asked again. I know because it has happened to me. A question popped up in my inbox, and I was able to respond with a link to a past blog post.

➤ Respond to questions found online

A follow-up suggestion to using your inbox to generate ideas is to use discussion groups or LinkedIn questions in the same way. People are asking questions in many areas, so find an inquiry that matches your knowledge and start writing. You can always go back to where you found the question and respond with a link to your blog post to drive a little more traffic and provide the answer. Once you start looking at questions other people have, you may find an overwhelming amount of potential blog posts.

➤ Read other sites

Another great content generator is reading industry news and other people's blog posts. You may find an interesting article or point of view upon which you can comment. Write some quick thoughts on it and post to your blog with a link to the original. Someone else's thoughts can often spur a flood of ideas. Use these ideas to share the information, expand on the idea with your own thoughts, or even to disagree with the other person's point of view.

➤ Provide links to articles you think your audience will find interesting

I read about my industry a lot and often find something that I think others might find interesting—so I share it. Over time, you will begin to learn what type of content your audience appreciates most so you can concentrate on finding that information. You'll likely come up with ideas for your own content as well.

➤ Start a conversation with a question

Give people an invitation to respond by asking a question. While you may not always get an answer, people will see that you are interested in learning more about your readers, not just talking to them. The question can be related to your business or can just be a fun diversion.

➤ Post a picture

Similar to a question, posting a picture will sometimes elicit more responses than words. It always helps if the picture is something cute or funny that engages your readers. Consider asking people to create a caption for the picture.

➤ Provide links to your posts

As you create blog posts or news releases, be sure to post links on your spokes. It gives people another way of knowing there is updated content. Some people use their social network connections like an RSS reader, so be sure to broadcast those links.

➤ Ask for feedback

Thinking about carrying a new product? Want to offer a new service but interested in some public opinion first? Just ask. Your community will be happy to provide feedback and ideas. Sometimes it will come unprompted, but often you will need to get the ball rolling.

➤ Provide a sample or discount

One of my clients was struggling to get people to leave comments and really engage. We knew people were reading the information, but they weren't necessarily responding. We decided to provide a sample to that specific group and instantly saw a change in behavior. People began to comment, post, and interact more. I'm not saying rewarding your community will work for everyone, but it is definitely worth considering.

➤ Provide a behind-the-scenes view of your company

Have you ever watched "Unwrapped" on the Food Network? It shows you how some of our favorite foods are manufactured. Do you have a process that you talk about with prospects? Now you can show it to them using video or photographs.

➤ Interview staff

Here's another behind-the-scenes idea. Interview staff and post their responses online, using video or a simple write-up of questions and answers. Mix in some fun to make it more interesting. Maybe even ask others for questions they would like to see answered. Providing a look into the personality of a company goes a long way.

➤ Interview clients

A written testimonial from a happy client is one thing, but a client taking the time to speak on camera is a completely different story. Video testimonials can be very powerful. Again, it does not need to be professionally shot, but you still need to prepare before getting in front of the camera.

The information you post does not need to be in text format only; be sure to include pictures, videos, and audio. Have fun and show the human side of your business. Remember: it is better to give than to receive. Share and pass on other people's information and they will return the favor.

Editorial calendar

The editorial calendar is a standard tool in the publishing business—and, quite frankly, you now have to think of yourself as a publishing business. Your products and services are the same, but as soon as you enter into social media, the editorial calendar can become your best friend. This tool is going to give you your roadmap for content for the upcoming month.

If you aren't a natural writer or are new to blogging, it's often difficult to come up with content ideas on the spot. I am especially challenged when I am busy and focused on my clients' projects. The editorial calendar forces you to sit down and look at the upcoming month and begin to fill it in with ideas for your blog as well as other marketing tools. Remember that your goal is to integrate. Look at your schedule for the upcoming month and see what happenings you can incorporate into your social media content.

The calendar will help you plan posts for both your hub and corresponding spokes. When things get hectic during the month, it's nice to have the calendar to help you stay prepared and produce fresh content. While it doesn't need to be overly detailed with daily updates, your calendar does need to contain the big must-do items.

One of my clients has multiple authors for her blog, with each one writing about many different topics. By using an editorial calendar, the authors know their deadlines so they can prepare their posts on time.

Your calendar can be done on a weekly or monthly basis. If you schedule beyond a month, it probably won't be as useful since you have to be flexible enough to account for unexpected news and trends. While you may not know the exact links you want to share, you may want to set a daily or weekly goal for posting.

Be prepared to make adjustments as you go since you will be evaluating what works and what doesn't. At first there will be a lot of trial and error—and, over time, your audience's needs may change as well. Be open to trying new things and abandoning those that are no longer effective.

➤ Advantages of using an editorial calendar

Here are just a few of the many ways you can use an editorial calendar to your advantage:

Write better posts

Increase the quality and quantity of your posts. Your calendar will help you stay focused on the goal of your blog, which will help increase the overall quality. By being organized with both the content type and frequency, you will be able to meet your quantity goal as well.

Be more productive

Instead of posting on the fly, you can take a chunk of time and collect links, posts, and relevant information to populate your calendar. One of the most productive things I can do with my blog is to set aside a block of time to consume and create content. If I sit down with my editorial calendar, I can produce several posts at the same time that I can then publish on designated dates. The result is better content, since I am not rushing to create a post just to get it onto the blog.

See the big picture

You are so close to your business that by stepping back and looking at the big picture you will be able to find useful information to share. When you are involved in your industry every day, all day, you may consider much of what you read to be basic knowledge. However, to others it is brand new and may be helpful and interesting. With an editorial calendar, you can look at things as an outsider, which brings you one step closer to providing great content to your audience.

Stay focused

An editorial calendar keeps you focused and on track when life gets hectic.

Integrate

Preparing your editorial calendar forces you to look at all areas of your business to see how you can integrate your marketing tools with your new social media strategy. Maybe you can link to some blog post from last month in your upcoming email newsletter to allow for exposure to your blog and recycle your content.

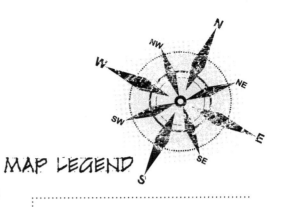

➤ Items to consider for your calendar

Upcoming events or tradeshows

The great thing about events is that they give you material to share before, during, and after. Before the event, promote the fact that you will be there, where you can be found, anything special you will be promoting, and invite your audience to stop by. During the event, mention people who have stopped by, upload pictures of the event in progress, and share the excitement that non-attendees are missing. After the event, provide a recap and share more photos or videos. Remember to create a <u>hashtag</u> for your event so you can track the conversation of others through the use of your monitoring tool.

Sponsorships

If you sponsor people or events, you have a lot of content that can be very useful and fun in social media. Treat the events as I described above. Keep your audience updated with the latest news and maybe exclusive interviews. Another great thing to do is encourage participants at the event to upload any pictures they take. These photos provide great content and get your community involved.

MAP LEGEND

HASHTAG is signified with a # and is used to tag specific content so you can track conversations throughout the Internet.

Holidays

Have some fun during holidays by asking questions and offering promotions. It doesn't have to be a major holiday. Maybe there is a holiday that ties into your business, like National Chocolate Chip Day for a bakery. (By the way, National Chocolate Chip Day is May 15!)

Seasonal items that affect your industry

Businesses with products that are offered on a seasonal basis can take advantage of unique content ideas. If you are a nursery, you can lead up to planting season with information about the correct time to plant and information on how to prepare your beds for planting.

What type of media to use throughout the month

Think about how you can include media other than text throughout the month. Will you be somewhere you can take great photos, or are you meeting with someone you could interview on video? Look at your upcoming appointments and you may find some great opportunities for multimedia content.

Number of posts per week

I'm a proponent of quality over quantity when it comes to posting, but if you have a goal for a number of posts each week it helps you stay on track. It also helps you determine what kind of posts you will want to write.

Demonstrations

Do you have a product or service that you can demonstrate either via a video or screencast of your computer? Providing a tip or showing a new use with a video could be very useful to your audience. Depending on what the video is, it could go viral like "Will It Blend" by Blendtec (http://www.blendtec.com/willitblend/).

Interviews that need to be scheduled

If you plan on posting interviews, you also need to add to your calendar when the interview will take place so you have enough time to edit and get it ready to post.

New products (arrivals and releases)

Do you expect any new product arrivals or will you be introducing any new services or products during the upcoming month? If so, include this information on the calendar. Consider offering a sneak peek to your community before the actual release.

New hirings

If there are new key hirings coming up, plan to announce that as well—especially if the new hire will be interacting with the public.

Other things to consider

Set up a type of post for days of the week. For example, every Monday is How To Monday. It helps you produce content, and your readers know what to expect week to week.

If it is a team blog, an editorial calendar allows the individual authors to see what they are writing about and when so they can incorporate it into their own schedules. If there is an approval process in place, put due dates on the calendar as well just to keep everyone on track. Back tasks out from the post date to create the workflow for the calendar.

Remember to add non-social media items to the calendar, such as press releases, ads, and email newsletters. Keeping everything integrated will help provide other topics for discussion.

Routine

In addition to your editorial calendar for creating content, I recommend setting up a routine for other day-to-day tasks—such as monitoring, commenting, sharing, and responding.

Here are some things to remember:

➤ Rule of three

You should check your social media accounts at least three times a day for any comments and/or posts to which you need to respond. My suggestion is to check them in the morning, before or after lunch, and again before heading home for the day. If people are trying to communicate with you via Twitter, Facebook, or other tools, you need to respond in a timely manner.

➤ Moderate comments

If you are going to moderate comments for your blog before they appear publicly, be sure to be near your computer after you put up a new post. You want comments to appear quickly to facilitate the conversation and keep your community involved. If you have a smartphone, look at getting a mobile application that allows you to moderate comments while on the road.

➤ RSS reader

Remember to include your RSS reader into your routine. By reading news and posts from others, you have opportunities to find content to share, as well as the ability to elaborate on that person's content with your own post. It's also great for content ideas for your editorial calendar. In addition, you want to include commenting on other people's blogs as part of your routine.

➤ Monitor alerts you find in your monitoring reports

Aim for once a day in case there is something that requires your immediate attention.

➤ Post to both your hub and spokes

The frequency is based on your editorial calendar. Like I said before, I like to set aside time to write several posts at the same time and then post them over time. It really takes the stress off my daily to-do list.

➤ Comment on other blogs

This task will likely become an extension of your reading, but you also will want to watch for posts from people you follow via your social networks. Stay involved with the blogs that make the most sense to your business, i.e. what your audience reads.

Get your groove back

Sometimes things just don't go as planned. Schedules and life get in the way. It happens to the best of us.

It happens to me more often than I care to admit. As a one-person company, I work on several projects at a time and often get swamped with deliverables and billable hours. It's difficult to justify taking the time to write a blog post or spend some time sharing links on Twitter and Facebook. I can get so knocked off my schedule that I can't even find my editorial calendar. Also, because I'm not a natural writer, after a few days it becomes easier and easier to lose my good habits. Here's how I get back on track:

First, I don't beat myself up—well, at least not for too long. What's done is done and behind me. I pick myself up, brush myself off, and get back to my plan. So my blog goes without a post for a few extra days; it's not the end of the world. I find when I write my first post after an interruption, it is usually a pretty good one.

Write something. Anything. It does not have to be on the subject of your blog or even a post at all. Write a letter or an email to a friend. Just take some time and get some words written down. I often use my personal blog for this purpose. I write about something I just baked or cooked in order to get my rhythm back. Once I am done there, I check my editorial calendar and get back to writing.

Read some news—and not just industry-related. I read a lot of social media sites and blogs, but I also read a lot of blogs not related to what I do. I like to see what is happening outside my bubble. I often find something that gets my brain clicking again. I can take something I read and transform it into a blog post. You never know what might spark inspiration. Remember to step out of your bubble.

Read and tweak your editorial calendar. I have a habit of being too aggressive with any schedule I make. I think I can do much more work than I have time to do. I often have to revisit my editorial calendar and do some tweaking to make it feasible with my current workload.

Social media is about consistency, but sometimes life intervenes. If you find yourself in this situation, take a deep breath and get back on the horse.

Etiquette

You learned how to "play nice" in kindergarten, but the same lesson bears repeating when it comes to social media:

➤ Remember to thank people

If people take the time to share your information with their own networks, try to take some time to thank them. Show them that they are important to you. Keep nurturing the people in your community. You may need their help some day.

➤ Be responsive

In addition to thanking people, be sure to respond to questions with an answer. So often companies will post something that elicits a response from the audience and then fail to follow up. Doing so makes it seem that you do not care about the person asking the question.

➤ It's better to give than to receive

Passing along other people's information and providing answers to questions can take you far in the world of social media. It's always been the right thing to do, but giving is the true currency in social media. It's not about giving a discount but rather showing you truly care about your community and not your own self-promotion.

➤ Join conversations, but be relevant

Don't jump in with irrelevant thoughts to the conversation, especially if they are heavily self-promotional. You are the expert at what you do and you can share some of that expertise without giving away free consulting. This information goes a long way and puts you at top-of-mind when someone has a need for your product or service.

➤ Limit your self-promotion

It's marketing, so of course the goal is self-promotion—but there is a limit. If you promote too much, you will be considered noise and be ignored. Be sure to mix your self-promotion with sharing other people's information and answering questions.

➤ Be respectful

My mother taught me at a young age that if you can't say anything nice, don't say anything at all. People will challenge you, and it is your job not to take it personally and be drawn into a fight. We've discussed trolls and how to handle negative comments, so you are prepared. You may be frustrated by something going on in your day and feel like posting a negative statement. Count to 10, take a deep breath, and really think about the ramifications. Be nice. You'll make your mom proud.

➤ Learn the language of each tool

Many social networks and tools have their own way of doing things and addressing people. Be sure to understand the semantics for each site you are involved in so that you communicate effectively on each platform.

➤ Don't repost the same information too many times

Not everyone in your network will see every post or status update you publish, so you may need to do it more than once during the day. Just be careful not to overdo it. I would say no more than once every 8 hours for a 24-hour period so your message is spread out and seen in all time zones. If it is an ongoing promotion, a few times a week is a good pace.

➤ Go beyond "just posting" and converse with people

The real power of social media comes from the conversations you have with people. Whether it is someone you know in real life (IRL) or someone you have met online, you never know where that connection may lead—maybe a new customer, partner, or referral. Don't just worry about promoting your information; have true conversations.

POTHOLES

CAUTION! Avoid:

➤ Forgetting what you put online is there forever.

➤ Not building social media into your routine.

➤ Not creating an editorial calendar

➤ Mass updating the same thing to all your spokes.

➤ Not learning the etiquette for each tool.

➤ Not responding to comments and questions.

➤ Forgetting that giving is better than receiving.

TALES FROM THE ROAD

WOW Logistics
www.wowlogistics.com

WHAT ADVICE WOULD YOU SHARE WITH OTHER BUSINESSES THAT ARE JUST GETTING STARTED WITH SOCIAL MEDIA?

Start with one tool. If you try to do them all too fast it will be overwhelming. Use whichever you feel is best for your business. It may be LinkedIn or Facebook or Twitter. Start small and grow from there—just like you did your business.

WHAT WAS YOUR BIGGEST FEAR BEFORE STARTING WITH SOCIAL MEDIA - AND WAS THE FEAR WARRANTED?

Not being noticed—being that small fish in the big pond of social media. Social media is what you make of it and size does not matter if you provide value to your readers.

PROMOTING YOUR SOCIAL MEDIA EFFORTS

Now that you're up and running with your hub and spokes, it's time to let people know where they can interact with you. This issue isn't new. When phones became popular, how did companies tell people about their phone numbers? They used business cards and the phone book.

When I started my business in 1999 and completed a website for a client, I would submit it to the search engines. In addition, I would advise clients to put their website URL any place they had their phone number, including business cards, print ads, direct mail, email signatures, and newsletters. Now when you look at almost any company's advertising materials, you see the URL.

Promoting your social media efforts is similar. Think about where your URL appears now and what the audience is for that source. Are you using a tool to reach that audience? If so, consider adding that tool's address to that marketing piece.

It's possible you will add several addresses. For example, on my business cards, I have my blog address and Twitter account name, in addition to my URL. When I get my next batch of cards printed, I will add my Facebook URL. Don't go overboard with trying to add every site; add the main ones that will also have links to your other sites.

Here's another suggestion for cross-promoting your social media efforts. On your blog or hub, you should have a link to every one of your spokes. If your spokes allow for multiple links, then link back to your hub and other spokes. If you can only have one link, make sure it is to your hub site. Most likely, the main goal of your spokes is to drive people to that hub. On your hub, the user can find the other links.

People are already visiting your website so you will want to put links in a prominent position and not just on your home page. Remember that people can enter your website from any page. A quick Google search will lead you to free icons for the most popular social media sites.

A simple yet effective promotional tool is including your links in your email signature. People have been adding contact information there for years, so now with a little update you can direct people to your new social media sites—an especially effective way to let current customers know about your new efforts.

If you are integrating social media into a specific campaign, be sure to include those links as part of the other pieces involved in the campaign. For example, if you are using YouTube as an extension of a print campaign, include the URL to your channel on the print ad. Consider doing so even if the social media tool has an ongoing strategy.

In addition to promoting your blog through your spokes, you can give your readers the ability to easily promote you through their spokes. Make it easy for your readers to share your content. The first way is when you tweet. Be sure to leave enough room so it can be retweeted easily and without edits. There are also several plug-in options to add sharing to your blog. The one that I use is called Socialble and is easy to install and configure. Facebook also provides many ways that your audience can easily share your content. These tools are great, but be careful not to add too many since it could cause your site to load too slowly. That will turn people away for sure.

If you exhibit at trade shows or speak at events, make sure your handouts contain the proper links. You may even want to create a postcard-sized handout specifically for this purpose. Its usefulness will extend beyond any single event.

I have found that a great way to build my online network is to attend events such as conferences, user groups, and tweetups. You will meet new people and often will find they are also active on one of your spokes. Get their account information, so you can connect with them online after the event. Staying in touch with people—even if it's only online—goes a long way toward building your community.

Another way to promote your social media efforts, especially your blog, is to get involved in other people's communities by commenting on other blogs. When you leave a comment on someone's blog, you also leave a link to your blog as part of your comment. Other people can then check out your blog if they feel you have left an insightful comment and want to learn more about you. Also as an author of a blog, I like to check out the blogs of my readers and add them to my reading list.

My word of caution here is to not treat other people's blogs as a billboard to promote yourself or your blog. Think of it as online networking. You are engaging in conversation with the author and other people who comment on that blog. Through regular conversation, you enhance relationships and thus readers, including those who may promote your blog through their spokes. Look for blogs that have the same kind of audience you want to attract to your site, in addition to those you learn from and those where you interact with peers.

Let's turn our attention to leveraging your current network, which may include:

- Friends

- Business associates

- Business partners

- Vendors

- Resellers

- Customers

- Newsletter subscribers

- Employees

CAUTION! Avoid:

➤ Not promoting your social media efforts outside of your social media tools.

➤ Not taking relationships offline by attending Tweetups, conferences, and meetings.

These people know you and are open to receiving your message—plus some of these groups may even be your target audience. It should be fairly easy to reach out to these groups. Let them know about your new efforts and invite them to engage with you there. The added benefit is that they will be able to promote it to their own networks, which can create quite the snowball effect.

Depending on the relationship, you may be able to promote each other's social media efforts—particularly when it comes to companies you work with, such as resellers, vendors, and partners.

I will add a caveat here: don't abuse your relationships just to increase numbers. Your friend may be wonderful and supportive but may not be interested in your product or service. Don't shame him or her into connecting with your business.

You want people in your community to want to get more information from you, which leads to better engagement and conversations. I would much rather have 50 really engaged and interested followers than 200 who never engage in conversation with me.

Remember, your social media efforts should extend your marketing, not replace it. Take advantage of all your marketing tools to cross-pollinate your message.

TALES FROM THE ROAD

New York Guest
www.newyorkguest.com

BIGGEST SUCCESS?

There have been many successes. The biggest was probably making the very first sale through social media efforts. That proved to us that it wasn't a waste of effort, time, and money... that we can really reach new clients through social media. In addition, we just hit the 10,000 Facebook follower milestone. That was a big celebration for me. For this small business to have 10,000 people following our content around the globe...how else could we achieve that measure?

WHAT DO YOU KNOW NOW THAT YOU WISH YOU'D KNOWN BEFORE YOU DELVED INTO SOCIAL MEDIA?

I wish I had known the importance of personalizing my content. At first, I thought to be the impersonal voice of the company was key. That sounded and seemed professional to me. However, I learned that people respond better to the voice of an actual person, so I have personalized the content more towards my own message and experience (though still relevant to our corporate themes).

MEASURING RESULTS

You are now working the plan you've created. So how do you know the plan is working? When you selected your tools, you were supposed to define your goal for using that specific tool. Now let's discuss how to measure your performance to see if you are achieving those goals.

Measuring performance in social media can sometimes be challenging because it is difficult to track the success of a conversation. Also, many people who consume your information through social media will not interact.

Tracking performance is not easy and can be time consuming. Try to find a system that works best for you so you have information on which to base decisions. Some of the following will work for you, but you may also find other options that suit your business.

➤ Goal: Increase traffic

What to measure: Number of visits to the site you want to measure

How to measure: Using analytics software, such as Google Analytics, you can measure the traffic to your website or blog. By looking at your analytic reports you can track the source of your visits to see which spoke has driven the traffic to your site or hub.

➤ **Goal: Increase awareness**

What to measure: Online mentions

How to measure: Through your listening post, you will track all mentions—positive or negative. An increase in mentions shows an increase in conversations and therefore awareness.

➤ **Goal: Thought leadership**

What to measure: Number of click-throughs, comments, and shared messages

How to measure: A click-through can be measured by using a URL shortener that tracks how many times someone has clicked on that link. These are popular on social networks where long URLs are unwieldy. (URL shortener: bit.ly)

Comments just need to be counted and can appear on social networks, your blog posts, and microblogging sites. Shared messages are most easily picked up by your monitoring but may also be tracked through the specific site where the information was found and shared.

➤ **Goal: Education**

What to measure: Number of click-throughs, comments, and shared messages

How to measure: Education is measured similar to thought leadership.

➤ Goal: Networking

What to measure: Number of meetings arranged

How to measure: Pretty obvious, right? If you schedule a meeting with someone you met through social media, you keep track of it and mark it as the source of contact.

➤ Goal: Better customer service

What to measure: Sentiment of mentions and direct feedback

How to measure: You can measure sentiment by reviewing your mentions. In addition to sentiment you should also look at your mentions to see if they reference customer service or another area of your business.

➤ Goal: Increase revenue

What to measure: Revenue

How to measure: As you go through the sales cycle from prospect to customer, ask your customers how they heard about your business. If it was from your social media activity, then make note of it in addition to the amount sold.

➤ Goal: Event promotion

What to measure: Attendees

How to measure: Similar to revenue, you will track sign-ups. It's easy to provide a way to sign up online that your community can only link to via your social media accounts.

➤ Goal: Customer feedback

What to measure: Responses

How to measure: When you ask for feedback, keep track of how many people respond over time. Is most feedback positive or negative?

➤ Goal: Word of mouth

What to measure: Number of mentions and how often information gets shared

How to measure: Monitor in the same way you monitor customer service, except you won't focus on just one area of the company.

➤ Goal: Customer loyalty

What to measure: Repeat purchase and redemption of specials

How to measure: Similar to tracking increase in revenue, you want to track returning customers. One idea is to offer an exclusive discount on one of your social media spokes and then track redemptions.

➤ Goal: SEO

What to measure: Keywords

How to measure: You have to know which keywords you want to rank highest. You can track the keywords used most frequently by looking at your site analytics report. Keep an eye on your analytics to see if visits to your targeted keywords increase.

➤ **Goal: Media relations**

What to measure: Press mentions

How to measure: Just like you used to keep your press clippings, your monitoring will produce similar information for your online press mentions. You will have to decide if you want to include bloggers or treat them separate from news sites.

Benchmark

You know what information you need to collect in order to measure success, but how will you determine if it truly is a success? You need to have a baseline from which to compare your new results. You may not have a lot of historical information for comparison, but you can probably make some assumptions and estimates to give you a head start. Like I said earlier in this book, you can't know where you are going if you don't know where you have been.

Now that you have your baseline and a few months of information regarding your social media efforts, it is time to evaluate. You really should wait three to six months before you can truly evaluate effectiveness. It takes awhile to build and nurture your community.

Also, when it is time to evaluate, only you can determine what kind of results you are looking for in order to define something as a success or failure. Once you have defined it as either a success or a failure, you will need to determine your next course of action.

You may be thinking that if it is a failure, then you will abandon the initiative. You could definitely follow that line of thinking—or you could determine if there is a different way to use the tool that could be more effective. You may want to change your audience or the type of content you are producing before completely moving on to different opportunities.

Now add the following to each tool you have implemented:

Tool name: _____

_____

How will I measure? _____

_____

What is my initial timeframe before evaluating success/failure? _____

_____

What is my benchmark? _____

_____

How will I determine success or failure? _____

_____

What will I do upon determination of success or failure? _____

_____

Moving forward

So there you have it. We have made it through the entire marketing process for engaging your audiences using social media tools. Feels good, right? There are just a few more things I want you to think about as you move forward so you can continue to be successful.

Continue to monitor. Keep an eye on your monitoring tool to look for any issues that you need to address, as well as any opportunities. Maybe there is a new blog on the block that requires your attention, or you may discover that your audience has found a new site they like to use.

Watch for new opportunities in technology. You need to evaluate new tools and sites to see if they make sense to add to your efforts.

Measure and adjust as needed. Keep measuring and evaluating effectiveness. Make adjustments when you need to and always listen to your community. You may find that they help you to define your content as time goes on. After all, it really is about them.

Last but not least, remember to be yourself and have fun. Social media should not be a major chore for you. If it is, your audience will be able to tell, based on how you interact with them—and it will turn them off. The tools will change, but the conversations will remain, so have some fun out there and do good things.

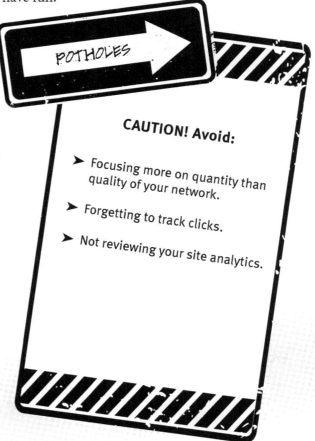

CAUTION! Avoid:

➤ Focusing more on quantity than quality of your network.

➤ Forgetting to track clicks.

➤ Not reviewing your site analytics.

TALES FROM THE ROAD

Griot's Roll Film Production & Services, Inc.
www.griotsrollproduction.com

WHAT ADVICE WOULD YOU SHARE WITH OTHER BUSINESSES THAT ARE JUST GETTING STARTED WITH SOCIAL MEDIA?

It is a building relationship tool; if you are going to do social media then leave the selling for off line and business lunches. Social media gets your foot in the door— a personal introduction into your target market.

Make sure that you have a clear vision on where you are going and what you want to accomplish online. Set goals for yourself; have a plan. Make sure that you have a target of friends you want on your pages, and keep your pages very professional with your logo on your page. Always remember that, although you are trying to build your business, you must be careful of what you say online. (Ex. I only accept friends who are business owners or entrepreneurs on Facebook.)

WHAT WAS YOUR BIGGEST FEAR BEFORE STARTING WITH SOCIAL MEDIA - AND WAS THE FEAR WARRANTED?

That social media was a trend that was going to fade and it was a big waste of manpower and time. That fear was not warranted. It helped my business build its brand and has gotten me opportunities that I didn't get through networking and going to business conferences.

APPENDIX A
SAMPLE SOCIAL MEDIA ROUTINE

Daily activities

These are activities that should be done daily. The specific activities you add to your personal routine depend on the tools you are using.

1. Check your listening post for mentions that require response.

2. Check Twitter at least three times a day for mentions and direct messages that need your response.

3. Tweet at least one time a day if using Twitter, preferably three times.

4. Check social networks you are active on at least once a day. If you recently posted something, try checking it three times a day.

5. Browse your RSS reader or other news sources for information to share.

6. Check your blog for comments. Remember to check your spam folder too.

7. Check your editorial calendar for items you need to complete.

Weekly activities

1. Publish blog posts at least once a week.

2. Publish posts to social networks two to three times a week.

3. Check your blog's analytics.

4. Check your RSS and email subscription numbers.

5. Set aside a chunk of time to create content.

6. Comment on other blogs two to three times a week.

Monthly Activities

1. Look at measurement numbers and evaluate results.

2. Create next month's editorial calendar.

3. Look for opportunities for new tools, strategies, or integration.

4. Look at website analytics.

Your routine

Based on your goals and tools, create your routine.

Daily

1. _____

2. _____

3. _____

4. _____

5. _____

Weekly

1. _____

2. _____

3. _____

4. _____

5. _____

Monthly

1. _____

2. _____

3. _____

4. _____

5. _____

APPENDIX B
EDITORIAL CALENDAR

Items to schedule

- Time to research and create content

- When content is due to editor

- When edited post goes to blog manager

- When to publish blog post

- If team blog, label who is author for each post

- Dates for social network posts

- Other marketing events or tools that take place during month

- When to create next editorial calendar

- Any other item you want to track

Sample calendar

Abbreviations *(you can create your own)*

CC – Content creation   FB – Facebook

E – Due to editor   TW – Twitter

B – Due to blog manager   A1 – Author 1

P – Publish blog post   A2 – Author 2

EC – Editorial calendar   N – Email newsletter

SUNDAY	MONDAY	TUESDAY	WEDNESDAY	THURSDAY	FRIDAY	SATURDAY
	CC – A1 FB TW	E TW	 FB TW	B – A1 TW	P FB TW	
	CC – A2 FB TW	E TW	 FB TW	B – A2 TW	P FB TW	
	CC – A1 FB TW	E TW	FB TW N	B – A1 TW	P FB TW	
	CC – A2 FB TW	E TW	 FB TW	B – A2 TW EC	P FB TW	

Remember:

- Your calendar will be different than this one. You need to customize it for your needs.

- Your calendar may change from month to month as you learn what works and what does not.

- You may want to try different days for blog posts to see when you attract the most traffic.

APPENDIX C
RECAP OF SOCIAL MEDIA STRATEGY

Target audiences

Make a list of the audiences you want to target, your goal in reaching them, and the message you wish to deliver.

Audience name: _____

Goal: _____

Message: _____

_____

Audience name: _____

Goal: _____

Message: _____

_____

Audience name: _____

Goal: _____

Message: _____

_____

Social media tools to use

Make a list of the initial social media tools you plan to use. Include the tool name, the overall goal you wish to achieve with each tool, the type of messaging you will deliver, and how you will measure for success. Lastly, note how often you hope to update each tool on a daily, weekly, or monthly basis.

Tool name: _____

Goal: _____

Type of message: _____

How to measure: _____

Frequency of updates: _____

Tool name: _____

Goal: _____

Type of message: _____

How to measure: _____

Frequency of updates: _____

Tool name: _____

Goal: _____

Type of message: _____

How to measure: _____

Frequency of updates: _____

Helper tools to use

List the helper tools, if any, that you will use for managing your social media strategy *(i.e. TweetDeck, bit.ly, Google Analytics).*

1. _____

2. _____

3. _____

4. _____

5. _____

Existing marketing tools to integrate

List any existing marketing tools you plan to use as part of your social media marketing strategy.

1. _____

2. _____

3. _____

4. _____

Response protocol

If you have created your own response protocol, outline the procedure here for quick access.

When to respond and how: _____

_____

Who is responsible for responding: _____

_____

Will we have a comment policy: _____

_____

What will the comment policy include: _____

_____

Internal usage policy

If you have created a policy for how your staff will use social media, outline the information here for quick access.

What to include in policy: _____

_____

How it will be communicated: _____

_____

Team responsibilities

Briefly outline who is responsible for each aspect of your social media strategy.

Content creation: _____

_____

Managing the tools: _____

_____

Technical aspects: _____

_____

Editing: _____

_____

Other: _____

_____

Routine

Define what tasks you need to complete as part of your new social media routine.

Daily tasks: _____

_____

Weekly tasks: _____

_____

Monthly tasks: _____

_____

Action items

List the items you need to complete to launch your social media strategy.

1. _____

2. _____

3. _____

4. _____

5. _____

6. _____

7. _____

8. _____

9. _____

10. _____

Listening post keywords

List the keywords you will use on your listening post to monitor conversations.

1. _____

2. _____

3. _____

4. _____

5. _____

6. _____

7. _____

8. _____

9. _____

10. _____

www.ingramcontent.com/pod-product-compliance
Lightning Source LLC
Chambersburg PA
CBHW080409060326
40689CB00019B/4189